Simon & Schuster

New York   London   Toronto   Sydney   New Delhi

DYLAN RATIGAN

GREEDY BASTARDS

How We Can Stop **Corporate Communists,**
Banksters, and Other **Vampires**
from **Sucking America Dry**

Simon & Schuster
1230 Avenue of the Americas
New York, NY 10020

First Simon & Schuster hardcover edition January 2012

SIMON & SCHUSTER and colophon are registered
trademarks of Simon & Schuster, Inc.

For information about special discounts for bulk purchases,
please contact Simon & Schuster Special Sales at
1-866-506-1949 or business@simonandschuster.com.

The Simon & Schuster Speakers Bureau can bring authors to your live event.
For more information or to book an event contact the Simon & Schuster Speakers
Bureau at 1-866-248-3049 or visit our website at www.simonspeakers.com.

Designed by Ruth Lee-Mui

Illustration credits: Cartoons courtesy of Jim Hunt; all other illustrations
courtesy of HINTERLAND.

Manufactured in the United States of America

10   9   8   7   6   5   4   3   2   1

Library of Congress Cataloging-in-Publication Data

Ratigan, Dylan.
    Greedy bastards : how we can stop corporate communists, banksters, and other
vampires from sucking America dry / Dylan Ratigan.
        p.   cm.
    1. United States—Economic conditions—2009–   2. United States—Economic
policy—2009–   I. Title.
    HC106.84.R38 2012
    330.973—dc23   2011048586

ISBN 978-1-4516-4222-3
ISBN 978-1-4516-4224-7 (ebook)

This book is dedicated to everyone
whose intention is to be part of the solution
and to my mother, Adrienne Ratigan,
who taught me that that is what life is.

Me, We

MUHAMMAD ALI

Contents

Trillion Dollar Vampires

Imagine an ordinary man so desperate that he decides to rob a bank. For years, he's worked a steady job, but when he loses that job, the only work he can find is as a part-time clerk in a convenience store. Still, he makes do. He cuts his expenses and relies on a little help from his family, though he hates to do so. Then he starts to develop health troubles. He's nearly sixty years old, and he needs foot surgery. He develops crippling back pain and a frightening bone protrusion sticking out of his chest. He can no longer lift the stock he is supposed to load onto the shelves at the store. Although he could move in with his sister, he doesn't want to be a burden, and he knows that she can't afford to pay for his health care out of pocket any better than he can. So what choices does he have? He goes into the local bank and slips the teller a note. It demands $1—and health care.

This is not a fantasy, and the man wasn't crazy. He was thinking clearly about a crazy situation. Jail, he realized, was the one place where he could get health care without bankrupting himself and his family. "Because he only asked for $1," Yahoo! News reported, "he was charged with larceny, not bank robbery. But he said that if his punishment isn't severe enough, he plans to tell the judge that he'll do it again. His $100,000 bond has been reduced to $2,000, but he says he doesn't plan to pay it." Jail, he said, was the best of his bad options.

That true story is one glimpse of a country going seriously wrong. Our unemployment is stuck near Depression levels, prompting outcries on both the left and the right. "We're well on the way to creating a permanent underclass of the jobless," wrote economist Paul Krugman in the *New York Times*. "One-sixth of America's workers—all those who can't find any job or are stuck with part-time work when they want a full-time job—have in effect been abandoned." In the *National Review*, Rich Lowry wrote, "The statistics tell a dire, but incomplete, story. We were built to work. When we want to and can't, it is an assault on our very personhood." But even as the assault continues, our politicians seem not to notice, or not admit, how this country has changed. As Peggy Noonan, former speechwriter for President Ronald Reagan, asked in the *Wall Street Journal*, "Do our political leaders have any sense of what people are feeling deep down? They don't act as if they do. I think their detachment from how normal people think is more dangerous and disturbing than it has been in the past."

If jobs are a bad deal, housing is worse. More than one in four houses are underwater, and that figure obscures how bad it's gotten in the hardest-hit states. According to data from CoreLogic, a private research company, 63 percent of all mortgaged properties in Nevada are worth less than the owners paid for them. In Arizona, it's 50 percent. In Florida, 46 percent. Lacking jobs or stuck in low-paying ones, unable to sell their homes and move somewhere more promising, many Americans find that now is truly the worst of times. The US Census Bureau says that 43.6 million of us are now living in poverty—that's more poor Americans than ever in the half century since records have been kept. Talk about a bad deal.

According to the Central Intelligence Agency (CIA), the US infant mortality rate is nearly twice as high as those of France, Japan, and Australia. In 2011, as food prices around the world continued to rise, the *New York Times* reported that 16 percent of Americans answered yes to the following question: "Have there been times in the past 12 months when you did not have enough money to buy food that you or your family needed?" Compared with over thirty other "advanced economy" countries, *New York Times* columnist Charles Blow found that the United States now ranks among "the worst of the worst" on measures such as income inequality, student performance on math tests, average life expectancy, and the percentage of our citizens in prison. No wonder that in a CBS News poll, 70 percent of Americans surveyed felt that the country was going in the wrong direction.

Even people who are used to feeling good about their lives are sensing the changes: the University of Chicago's General Social Survey found that in 2010, only 29 percent of men and women reported being "very happy"—the lowest level of very happy people since the poll was first conducted in 1972.

But if this is the worst of times for many, it is an explosively wealthy time for a fortunate few. While jobs, investment capital, and confidence in the future drain away, there is good cheer in corporate boardrooms. According to a 2011 survey by the Business Roundtable, an association of chief executive officers from leading US companies, American CEOs felt more confident than ever before. And why shouldn't they? A survey by Equilar, a private research company specializing in compensation, found that median pay for CEOs in 2010 had risen to $10.8 million: an astonishing 23 percent pay raise compared with just the year before. How about you? Did you get *your* extra 23 percent last year?

The fact is, the very rich are doing very, very well, as they have been for two or three decades. Journalist Robert Frank, the *Wall Street Journal*'s first full-time correspondent about the very rich, found that "the United States is now the world leader in producing millionaires—even if it lags behind China and India in other kinds of manufacturing." Their demand for servants has raised butlering, once a dying career, into one of American's fastest growing trades, along with maids, nannies, personal assistants, and private security guards.

Butlering is one of our notable growth industries. It's not supposed to be like this. The United States is still a wealthy country. Wealth in a capitalist country is supposed to be invested, making new ventures possible, turning our ingenuity into new industries, creating jobs, and helping the economy grow. In the phrase that

President John F. Kennedy used often, a rising tide lifts all boats. But something has gone wrong in America. For the last few decades, the rising tide has been lifting only the yachts.

Almost anywhere you look, if you just open your eyes, you will see ordinary, hardworking people struggling. Not far away, you'll find a few greedy bastards making out like bandits. What defines greedy bastards? It's not merely that they're rich. I'm a capitalist; I am in favor of making lots and lots of money, as long as it comes from creating value for others. Americans have a long tradition of getting rich by making a great product or service that contributes to the growth of our country. But greedy bastards have given up on creating value for others and instead get their money by rigging the game so that they can steal from the rest of us.

Do You Suffer from Greedy Bastards?

Do you have greedy bastards in your state? In your congressional district? In your workplace? Are greedy bastards supplying your supermarket? Your big box stores? Are they lurking at your doctor's office, your hospital, your gas station, your power company, your elementary school, your local college? If you have an infestation of greedy bastards, you need to be able to see them. You need to know how they got in, and you need to know what actions to take to get them out.

So what do we do about all these greedy bastards?

That question has obsessed me since 2008, when the banking crisis hit. At the time, I was hosting the financial news show *Fast Money* on CNBC. I'd made a career as a financial news anchor and reporter, chatting up the big traders and billionaire CEOs, and breaking the stories that helped investors pick the right stocks to buy and sell. My success in financial journalism was due in large part to the many personal relationships I'd built with the business leaders I interviewed, such as Carl Icahn, Mohamed El-Erian, and Bill Gross. Shortly after the federal bailout deal was reached in 2008, I had lunch with a banking CEO who asked if he could speak off the record. He said, "Dylan, do you see what is going on here? This is the largest theft and cover-up in American history."

I didn't have to take his word for it. My then thirteen years of financial reporting were my education in the ways that business can build up or tear down a country, and the most important thing I ever learned was that if you want to understand where a country is headed, you have to follow the money. So I followed the money trail, and I discovered that many bankers are no better than gangsters, shaking down the American people. As I explain in chapter 2, "The World's Biggest Ongoing Heist," the theft was the banksters' ability to sell bad insurance on loans and keep the income even when they failed to pay legitimate claims. The cover-up was the government's choice to print trillions of dollars in new money to make it seem (for a while) as if the problem had been fixed.

It was true: the financial crisis and bailout were indeed the biggest theft and cover-up ever seen. Greedy bastards are making almost unimaginable fortunes by skimming money from the customers they are supposed to serve and giving virtually nothing in return. And then those same greedy bastards get more taxpayer money to keep the scam going.

My private conversations with top business leaders encouraged me to trust my own eyes. So while many business journalists were cheering the government for our latest "rescue" from crisis, I was calling for the government's supposed heroes to go to prison. As a guest on *The View*, I said that the politicians who authorized the bailout should go to jail. On the *Today* show, I accused AIG, the insurance company that received an $85 billion bailout, of blackmail. At first, most people in the media business thought I was straight crazy. They couldn't believe that I was saying this stuff. Many of the companies I was calling out were the ones buying the commercials that paid for financial news programs like mine. So I left *Fast Money*, started *The Dylan Ratigan Show*, and I kept talking. Because what makes me so angry, even today, is that *the underlying problems have not been solved*. The banksters are still using their sway with politicians to commit mind-boggling theft. Ordinary Americans are still being fleeced. All that the supposed rescue did was to shift the cost of their reckless gambling from the wealthy and powerful who had created the problem to ordinary people on Main Street.

I realized that our banking system, on which every business and every one of us depends, has become a greedy bastard's delight. Instead of serving its customers, it feeds on them. Vampires feast on blood, weakening and eventually killing their victims, but greedy bastards extract the lifeblood of countries, which is capital: the money, resources, and human potential that must flow through the body politic to nourish a nation's health and growth. When our capital is drained away to private bank accounts and foreign investment, the country becomes weak and sick, threatening our investments, our jobs, our homes, and our future as a great nation.

In a vampire industry, all the usual rules and incentives of good business are reversed. Instead of trying to provide the highest quality product to serve the customer best, a vampire industry preys on its customers. Rewards go not to whoever competes best, but to whoever cheats best. In a vampire industry, the most successful employee is not the one who is most productive, but the one who is greediest. If the job descriptions were honest, they would say, "Wanted: greedy bastards. Responsibilities: to take our customers' money any way you can."

Greedy bastards don't make money at all. They just take it. Here's what I mean:

If I start a venture capital firm that lends out money to drug researchers trying to find new cures for disease, and I get rich doing it, then I made my money by investing in the productive future of this country; I used my money in a way that facilitated scientific innovation and a cure. I'm what director of the Havas Media Lab Umair Haque calls a "capitalist who makes." But if instead I take the same money and use it to lobby for changes in a government regulation—changes that help me trick a union into investing its retirement savings in flawed investments so that I can collect the commissions—then I may move as many dollars into my bank account as someone who funded cures for diseases, but I haven't *made* anything. I'm a "capitalist who takes," exploiting my power to influence the government for my own private gain, no matter the harm to anyone else. I'm a greedy bastard.

In my reporting, I found banking overrun with greedy bastards, but banking was just the beginning. As I followed the money trail—the flow of capital through the body politic—I found multi*trillion*-dollar theft, perpetrated every day not just by banksters but also by greedy bastards in international trade, energy, health care, education, *and* by the politicians they buy. As I explain in chapters 3 through 6, we are borrowing from future generations to help send our jobs and our most productive industries to China. We have the least efficient energy industry in the developed world, wasting more than two-thirds of all the fuel we use. We have the least efficient health care industry in the world, paying up to seven times what some other countries pay for the same level of care. We spend more than almost anyone else on education, but our results are heartbreaking.

These industries were not always corrupt and wasteful. They once wanted many of the same things that the people did. There was a time in the past century when each industry was essential to our nation's progress. As Josh Fox, creator of the 2010 documentary *Gasland* told us on *The Dylan Ratigan Show*, "Oil and [gasoline] built the whole last century. We have them to thank for that." But the economic and environmental damage from our reliance on twentieth-century fuels is too severe for us to continue relying on an outdated energy industry. The same is true of finance, trade, health care, education, and politics. Each one had a productive life, and, as I'll explain, with the changes of the digital revolution, each should have died a natural death. But instead of making room for the new industries of the twenty-first century, they refused to die. They became undead, preying on the customers they used to serve.

In the original *Dracula* by Bram Stoker, it took a long time for people to realize that actual vampires walked among them. Count Dracula dressed elegantly and carried himself like royalty. People were slow to believe in the vampires' dark magic, which allowed them to move in secret, to hypnotize and control their servants, and to drain their victims' blood while keeping them from feeling the terrible cost. Today's vampire industries, too, have a dark magic: an unholy alliance with government based not just on the money that they contribute to political campaigns and spend on lobbying but on their ability to hypnotize us with false prices. How can a price be false if we pay it and they accept our payment? When the price we're aware of paying is only the first cost we have to bear, and there is a second, hidden cost that is far higher, I call this the Very Bad Deal hypothesis. It works like this.

First, a greedy bastard offers us a low price on something we want or need. We accept the deal—but there's a catch. Along with this thing we want, we have to accept a tiny chance that something terrible will happen. Here's where it becomes a Very Bad Deal: even though, on any given day, there is only a tiny chance that the Very Bad Thing will occur, in the long run the terrible thing is certain. It's as if we were offered a delicious candy bar, usually expensive, at a low price. The catch is that what makes the low price possible is that somewhere in each candy bar is a rock hard enough to break your teeth. You can't see the rock, and there is no way to figure out where it is. Any given bite of the candy bar is tasty and sweet, but every bite increases the chance that you will bite down on the rock. By the time you finish, you will surely hit the rock—and the greedy bastards will take little or no responsibility for the harm you suffer.

In this book, I will show you the worst of the Very Bad Deals and their hidden costs. I explain how our banking system gives us cheap credit for buying houses and cars and flat-screen TVs, and our trade relationships give us cheap imports from China, but if we continue to rely on these Very Bad Deals, we will wind up so deep in debt that our economy will be permanently crippled. I will show that the price of gasoline in America, which is far lower than in Europe or Asia, seems like a great deal, but if we continue to rely on our current energy system, our country will wind up bankrupt, badly polluted, and mired in endless wars. In these industries and more, as I will explain, the profits go to the greedy bastards, but the costs when they come due are paid by the government—that is, by taxpayers like you and me. I may enjoy that delicious, inexpensive candy bar, but my taxes will go up to cover my reconstructive dental work. In the end, that cheap candy will be the most expensive treat I ever bought. Talk about a bad deal.

In each of these bad deals, the hidden price we pay keeps going up as the value of the product we receive goes down. This is known in technical terms as an *outrageous rip-off*. Where is all that wasted money going? Some of it is lost: burned off or thrown away. The rest can be found in the pockets of the greedy bastards. They are the well-paid servants of the vampire industries.

When someone goes to an emergency room, the first medical professional he or she sees conducts triage, identifying which patients' conditions are the most serious, so that they can be treated first. It's time to conduct some honest triage on the United States of America. The truth is that we have been living with several massive, outdated industries. We all depend on them, but they are vampires that no longer give us what we want. We want clean domestic energy, but we get dirty imported energy. We want to grow our economy through international trade, but instead we're trading away our long-term economic assets and our jobs while our manufacturing economy shrinks. We want education that prepares all our young people for the future, but we get educational resources concentrated on a wealthy few. These are our most urgent problems because they endanger us the most.

Extractionism

Greedy bastards often call themselves capitalists, but what they are doing is the opposite of capitalism. Call it "extractionism": taking money from others without creating anything of value, anything that produces economic growth or improves our lives. In an extractionist system, you actually lose value at an increasing rate over time. Instead of giving people incentives to make good deals where both sides can benefit, the system rewards those who take and give nothing in return. Such people are commonly known as thieves. Sadly, America and many other countries across the globe have adopted extractionism as their chief economic policy, building it into our present systems for everything from trade and tax policies to banking.

If we don't deal with the rock in our candy bar—that is, trillion-dollar vampires—all our talk about the million-dollar and even billion-dollar problems will ultimately be futile. Right now, it's as if the United States is a vampire's victim brought to the ER by her family (the political parties). They tell the doctor, "She's pale! She's weak! She's in pain!" The Democrats want to get her a blood transfusion, to renew her strength and return the color to her face. The Republicans want to post armed guards outside her door day and night so that no one can attack her. They argue. They accuse.

The media reports that the Democrats have asked for another transfusion, but the Republicans won't pay for an additional pint of blood. But the problem is not bleeding or pain. Those are effects. The *cause* is vampire industries. We must stop these vampire attacks, because armed guards outside the door don't keep Dracula from turning into a bat and entering through the window, and transfusions just offer him dessert. We must stop wasting our time debating symptoms and bogus Band-Aid solutions while the trillion-dollar vampires have their teeth in our necks.

Let me be honest. It can be upsetting, especially at first, to think that we face so many challenges, and each one of them so big. I remember feeling discouraged when I realized that we had so many different trillion-dollar problems to solve. Weren't these problems complicated and difficult? Where could we find solutions to all these different problems? As Representative Ron Paul of Texas told me, "I think people are in denial, and maybe they don't want to think about the hard choices and don't want to think about how bad things are." But the more I investigated the greedy bastards that have overrun this country, the more *encouraged* I became. Why? Because I went looking for people with solutions, and I found that solutions are abundant.

One of the great things about my job is that people all over the world talk to me about the alternatives they've discovered and the methods they're testing. New digital technologies have made it easier for innovators to discover what works and to partner up to make good solutions even better. For instance, how to make our banking system more accountable and productive; how to generate cheaper, cleaner energy that doesn't leave us dependent on our enemies; how to provide better health care at lower cost; and so on down the list, with inspiration at every turn. The United States already has amazing innovators with solutions ready to implement. The real problem isn't finding solutions. The real problem is that the status quo is so profitable for greedy bastards that they do all they can to prevent these new solutions from being implemented. But I am optimistic because that means we have only one root problem: breaking the grip of the vampire industries so that we can restore American prosperity.

I wrote this book as a manual to stop the greedy bastards: how to recognize vampire industries, how to fight them, how to rescue their victims, and maybe even how to turn the greedy bastards from their destructive ways.

Storybook vampire hunters wield stakes and silver bullets, garlic and crucifixes. Those who fight to break the grip of any vampire industry have their own weapons: four core values acronymed *VICI*. These principles, which I think almost anyone in this country could share, have the power to turn bad deals into good ones:

Visibility,

Integrity,

Choice,

Interests.

Any deal or relationship, whether involving a business, a government, or even a family, that does not conduct itself according to these values will be prone to greedy-bastard behavior: secrecy, cheating, and exploitation of those it is meant to serve. But any organization or group of people that is true to these four values can triumph over corruption and free its full creative powers to generate success and prosperity. *Vici* is the Latin word for "I overcame," or "I prevailed." The VICI code is not just a set of separate values. Each one naturally leads to the next. Shared visibility brings about price integrity; with integrity of choice and prices, we can better align our interests around shared goals and values. Let's look at the VICI values one at a time, and how living by this code of values can help us overcome greedy bastards wherever we find them.

VISIBILITY. There is a reason why vampires like the dark: they prefer to move unseen and act with the advantages of secrecy and surprise. In the same way, vampire industries prefer opaque environments. Rigged prices, misaligned interests, and lack of choice are most effective when victims *can't see* that they're being controlled. But the best chance for those victims is to help turn on the lights, refuse the numbing drug of distraction, and recognize that they are dealing with greedy bastards who win when they lose. Visibility makes the other three values possible.

INTEGRITY. Imagine that you're in a store and comparing the prices for the merchandise on the shelves. You purchase an item, but when you get home, you discover that you've been overcharged. You've been cheated. The store has acted without integrity. Now imagine that every object in your life—the chair you might be sitting in, the electricity in your home, your last medical bill, the interest rate on your credit cards (even this book in your hands)—was also priced wrong. As I'll show, that's exactly the situation we face. The prices we pay are so manipulated by the unholy alliance between greedy bastards in business and the politicians they buy that we can't tell the real value of anything.

How can that be? Say that I own an old car powered by a gasoline engine. Maybe I've started to wonder if my next car should run on electricity or on flex fuel such as ethanol. Like many people, I'll make that decision based on price. If gas is cheap, I'll stick with the good deal I already have. If it's more expensive, I might switch. I use price to judge what things are worth, and I base many of my most important decisions on it.

But what if the price per gallon that I see posted at the pump is actually $10 too low because the oil companies used their influence with politicians to arrange subsidies, tax breaks, and other market controls? Now the government pays the additional $10 per gallon and then passes the bill on to the taxpayers. In that case, the free market can't help me decide if it's worth switching from gas to another fuel, because the market isn't free, it's rigged. My best attempts to compare prices so that I can make an informed decision about what car to buy will come out wrong, because the prices I use to make my choices are inaccurate. Without price integrity, I can be tricked into spending my money in ways that benefit greedy bastards, because I don't actually know the price I'm paying. But if I can learn how the prices have been distorted, then I can restore integrity to the system and make smarter decisions as a consumer.

CHOICE. The difference between a victim in the hands of a predator and a free agent in a fair market comes down to choice. If I have only one way to get the health insurance I need or a quality education for my children, then I will pay any price. Economists call this scarcity power: if you can make the thing that I need scarce, then you have the power to make me pay whatever you ask. No choice. And as a rule, any situation where there are very few choices—a handful of extremely similar employer-based health plans, two and a half domestic car companies, two functional political parties—breeds greedy bastards. True choice, on the other hand, creates competition and drives away the greedy bastards.

INTERESTS. People can work together productively only if their interests are aligned. If I'm on a pro basketball team, I may not like all of my teammates. I may not agree with everything the coach says. But if we are all interested in winning, then we will play together as productively as we can. However, if a few players get paid off by gamblers to throw the game, then our interests are no longer aligned. Some of us will play to win and some will play to lose. We will be far less effective. In the same way, if bankers receive bonuses for keeping the banking system running efficiently, they will work as a team to keep the banking industry productive. But if they know that they are going to receive enormous bonuses even when they corrupt the system, then the interests of the bankers and the interests of the rest of us—who need a reliable, effective banking industry—are not only out of alignment, they're in direct opposition.

Greedy bastards are people whose interests are not aligned with those they claim to serve: their only interest is to take as much as they can, as fast as they can, for themselves. But if an organization can get its interests back into alignment—for example, if banks refused to give bankers bonuses when they fail—then it can motivate more productivity. If bankers can make money only when they help society solve problems, then that is what will happen *because it is the only way bankers make money.*

Even better, if loans and investments offered the highest payouts when they created the most value as opposed to taking the most risk, we can create win-win deals. This is the true intention of the capitalist system: win-win deals where wise investment creates opportunity, innovation, and valuable goods and services.

Every Problem Is an Opportunity

Once I got past the initial shock of admitting that our country is in the grip of greedy bastards, I didn't feel discouraged. In fact, I actually felt optimistic, because for the first time, I could see the problem that ties everything together: the bad deal we are getting from the misaligned interests all around us. Only if we learn to recognize it in our day-to-day lives can we set about the business of coming together to change it.

I'm optimistic even when I see the massive waste and the ongoing theft perpetrated every day, because when I see that so much of our resources goes to bad deals, I realize how much we still have to work with—if we can redirect the resources of this great country. We do that by ending the bad deals in finance, taxes, and trade, in the process releasing trillions of investment dollars into energy, health care, education, and so on.

We have the chance to spend far less and get far more for it. We have a great collection of innovative talents—frustrated now by legacy industries that squeeze them out, but eager to put their ideas into practice. We have a vast workforce—underemployed now, but ready to get to work solving our real problems. What we need is to recognize the true dimensions of the challenge we face and align ourselves with the VICI code, to meet that challenge with resolve. The truth will set you free—but first it will piss you off.

2

The World's Biggest Ongoing Heist

Were you okay with the new banking tax? I'm talking about the increase in debt taken on by every American after the financial crisis of 2008. Simon Johnson, former chief economist of the International Monetary Fund (IMF), estimates it at roughly $3 trillion, or about $12,000 per US citizen. We could argue about that number, but I think we would all have to agree on three things. First, it is an enor-

mously high price. Second, the American taxpayer is paying it. And third, the government and the bankers don't call it a tax. But when taxpayer money pays for government activity, that's a tax, isn't it? So were you content with the massive new banking tax?

To answer that question, you would probably want to know what the bailout money bought. If it ended the crisis, held accountable those who created the problem, and fixed the system so that it wouldn't collapse again, it just might have been worth it. Unfortunately, as I'll show, we accomplished only one out of the three objectives. The immediate threat—the impending collapse of the entire financial system back in 2008—was halted. But the banksters and politicians responsible for exploiting the system are still doing exactly what they were doing before. No one was held responsible, and the system remains broken.

We are still stuck with a financial system that has become, essentially, a secret casino where the world's wealthiest companies and individuals bet with trillions in other people's money—*our* money—exempted from the laws that the rest of us have to follow. The winning gamblers keep all of the profits for themselves, while the government and the people pay the losses. "Increasingly now, Wall Street is an island unto itself, separate and distinct from the real economy," said Senator Bernie Sanders of Vermont. "They produce worthless, illegal products that nobody understands, make huge amounts of money for themselves, and when their Ponzi scheme collapses, they've got the American taxpayer bailing them out."

But what exactly is it that makes Wall Street's island so different from ours? To understand what's gone wrong with the banking and investment system and why all of us are paying so much to get so little, let's start by looking at how any banking system works, using the board game Monopoly as an example.

If you, me, and some friends want to play Monopoly, what's the first thing we do? Before anyone rolls the dice, we assign one player to be the banker, a part-time job. He or she hands out the $1,500 we each start with: two $500s, two $100s, two $50s, and so on. Without cash, players couldn't buy Baltic Avenue, Marvin Gardens, and the board's other properties. Our limited bank accounts force us to win on the strength of our scrutinized investment choices and some degree of luck.

The bank does not compete in the game; it is akin to a utility, like electricity or water. But in the actual financial system, the utility that was supposed to make it possible for the players to play the "game" not only competes against the other players but also does so with unlimited reserves of money.

To understand just how bad it's gotten, you have to know how our financial system worked at its best and how it has changed over the last few decades. It has devolved from a mainly functional utility with *some* cheating at the edges to a rigged casino where cheating is the main game. So let me take you in my financial time machine on the dizzying journey from the simple home mortgage to the financial regulations facilitated by Treasury Secretary Bob Rubin, President Bill Clinton, Federal Reserve chairman Alan Greenspan, Deputy Treasury Secretary Larry Summers, Texas senator Phil Gramm, and a few others in 1999 and 2000.

Although deregulation of the banking system has led to financial collapse, at the time, the instituted changes were sold as wise moves to free up investment capital and productive potential. The idea was to create what I think of as a "supercharged economy," not to lead us down the pathway of economic collapse. The safe, helpful, boring local bank gave rise to a lucrative breeding ground for greedy bastards like nothing the world had ever seen.

Leverage: America's Financial Speed Limit

Let's travel back to 1947. With the end of World War II, there was a huge demand for homes for returning soldiers and the families they were starting. One building firm, Levitt & Sons, adapted high-speed construction techniques developed for military housing and began using them to build suburban rental homes that proved popular. When the company announced a new suburban housing community, it rented a thousand homes in two days. The houses were for rent, not for sale, because veterans generally lacked the money for a down payment. And despite the builder's success, Levitt and other companies lacked capital—that is, the cash to buy the land and materials needed to build more homes faster—thus limiting their growth. As a result, the US economy could not provide its returning veterans with homes.

The government and banks stepped in by way of the Federal Housing Authority, an agency established by Congress in the midst of the Great Depression. As described by Kenneth T. Jackson in *Crabgrass Frontier: The Suburbanization of the United States,* the FHA provided builders with the cash flow they needed to expand production and insured thirty-year home mortgages up to 90 percent. Now veterans could buy homes with just a small down payment and a monthly mortgage payment of $58—about as much as they would have paid in rent. The housing development, on Long Island, was renamed Levittown, and by 1951, it included almost eighteen thousand homes. In time, other Levittowns were built in Pennsylvania, New Jersey, and Puerto Rico, and the Levittses' general vision of affordable ranch-style homes influenced the growth of suburbia nationwide.

This was not charity. The residents of Levittown paid back their mortgages, just as the builders paid back their production advances. But builders never could have scaled up production to meet the demand, and many of the veterans never could have become home owners if the banks and the government hadn't acted something like the bank in Monopoly—making it possible for players to start the game. In this way, the federal government's decision to use taxpayer money to make "commitments" to the builders and insure mortgages helped the banking system to serve the overall economy with aligned interests. Construction and sales took place immediately. The builders became wealthier from the homes they sold, while the home owners were able to build equity in their homes rather than only paying rent.

In general, the traditional bank that offered mortgages and small-business loans benefitted the national economy in two ways. First, it provided liquidity: opportunities were not wasted for a lack of cash, meaning that the market became more efficient. Second, it helped to ensure two VICI values: the integrity of prices for homes and for loans, and aligning the different parties' interests.

Think of any traditional mortgage. The home buyer wants to buy the house today rather than wait decades until he has saved up enough to buy it outright. The bank is then paid back with interest. The bank is betting that in the future the buyer will have the means to pay back the loan, so it is motivated to scrutinize the buyer for creditworthiness. The buyer also puts up the house as collateral: if he can't pay off the loan, the bank will keep the house. For their own self-interest, bankers traditionally had to act as what we might call "price integrity police," working to price loans, houses, and businesses correctly, and helping to improve the integrity of the entire system. Meanwhile, it was in the buyer's self-interest to pay back the loan; otherwise he could lose his house. The banking system helped align the self-interests of all sides to encourage the productive movement of capital through the economy; this was a key to American prosperity.

Moving capital through the body politic is so important, in fact, that the government grants banks a list of unique privileges available to no other industry by giving them a special federal charter. To put it another way, the foundation of Wall Street is special legal privileges and access to taxpayer money that the government gives banks so that Wall Street can provide crucial services for the national economy.

Among other benefits, banks that meet the requirements for a federal charter can borrow money from our central bank, the US Federal Reserve, at the lowest possible interest. Today, they do this and then immediately lend the money back to our Treasury to help finance everything our government does. Think of this arrangement as banks collecting rent on America. The banks are given trillions at our central bank. They then lend the same money back to the US Treasury Department at 3 percent interest. In this manner, the borrowed money is used to run the government, funding everything from tax loopholes, to war, to Medicare. The banks' new deal is as close as a business can come in the real world to being handed nearly limitless amounts of money by the Monopoly banker at the start of the game. If you're wondering how America's finances go wrong, this is the central locus of distortion. State banks give private banks money so that private banks can give the state their own money back for a fee.

What Went Wrong?

From the end of the Great Depression and into the 1980s, America enjoyed a largely functional banking system that contributed to national productivity and prosperity. Many of the same banks that had been overrun by greedy bastards before the regulatory changes of the Depression, and that were overrun again in the 1990s, were productive members of the financial society in between. Even Matt Taibbi, the *Rolling Stone* investigative journalist famous for describing Goldman Sachs as "a great vampire squid wrapped around the face of humanity, relentlessly jamming its blood funnel into anything that smells like money," acknowledged that "during the 1970s and 1980s, Goldman ... had a reputation for relatively solid ethics and a patient approach to investment that shunned the fast buck." The firm's mantra was "long-term greedy." One former Goldman banker who'd left the firm in the early nineties explained to Taibbi, "We gave back money to 'grown-up' corporate clients who had made bad deals with us. Everything we did was legal and fair— but 'long-term greedy' said we didn't want to make such a profit at the clients' collective expense that we spoiled the marketplace."

But if the traditional banking industry helped ensure the VICI values of price integrity and aligned interests with borrowers and investors, it was much weaker on visibility and choice, which, even in the old days, meant that bankers made a lot of easy money and consumers often endured a moderate amount of cheating (extraction of capital).

For example, when it came to buying and selling stocks, the consumer had no choice but to use a stockbroker. Brokers set two prices, the "bid" and the "ask": the price they were willing to pay for a given stock at a given time (the bid) and the price at which they would sell it (the ask). Stock market tradition held that stocks were sold in eighths of a dollar (the old stock charts listed prices in fractions—12⅛, 12¼, 12⅜, 12½—not decimals), and so brokers would always set their bid and their ask at least an eighth of a dollar apart, meaning that they made at least twelve and a half cents for every share they sold or bought for a client. Not surprisingly, since they had the power to maintain this old pricing tradition, and consumers had no choice but to accept it, stockbrokers made out quite well.

Bond brokers also did well. Not only couldn't consumers buy bonds without them, but also there was little transparency in the market. Imagine that it's 1974, and you manage a pension fund for teachers, say, in the state of North Carolina. You know that with the number of retired teachers in your state, you will need to send out $1 billion in pension payments each year. So you call up a firm that deals in bonds in New York and say that you want to make a bond investment that will pay you $1 billion annually in interest, which you are counting on for the teachers. What will it cost to make this investment, and what kind of bonds can it offer? The broker who answers the phone will probably say, "Hang on a minute," puff his cigarette, and run down the hall to open an enormous book that lists bonds and their yields. There are no computers in the office, and you, back in North Carolina, with the phone pressed to your ear, have no way to see the book. The system has no visibility.

The broker looks up the price. Then he goes to his boss, the head of the trading desk, and says, "There's a teachers' fund manager in North Carolina who wants an investment that will pay him a billion a year to pay the teachers' pensions."

The head of the trading desk says, "This guy's down in Raleigh playing golf; what does he know? Mark it up ten percent."

The trader gets back on the phone and quotes you the price, and you have to take it or leave it.

What I've described was the general state of the American banking system between the end of the Depression and the rise of the digital age: functional when it came to price integrity and alignment of interests, but with a lot of skimming around the edges.

Digital Crushes Profit Margins

Historically, American bankers were well-educated, well-connected men whose families went to the same summer camps, the same East Coast prep schools, and the same Ivy League colleges. They were accustomed to wealth and power, and they took it for granted. But the computer age threatened the bankers' comfortable world. By the mid-1980s, Bloomberg LP computer terminals offered bond buyers the same statistical information about bond prices and performance that bond dealers had always kept to themselves. Now that pension fund manager in North Carolina could subscribe to a Bloomberg terminal and be privy to the same information as that bond broker in New York. Once computers improved visibility, buyers could see exactly how much profit the bond dealers were making and demand lower markups. Suddenly there was greater choice for the consumer, but less easy money to be made as a bond dealer.

In the stock market, "decimalization" came in stages, but by 2001, the New York Stock Exchange was fully computerized, and the traditional spread for stockbrokers was gone. With the flick of a switch, as *Forbes* magazine reported, trades that had paid twelve and a half cents per share now might pay as little as a penny, because computers did not respect the old tradition of pricing in fractions no smaller than an eighth of a dollar. That cut stockbrokers' commissions by more than 90 percent. Even more damaging, online brokerage sites such as E*Trade offered consumers fixed rates per trade rather than charging a commission on every share bought or sold. Most significantly, they enabled buyers to trade from their home computers, without going through a human broker. Fewer stockbrokers were necessary to keep the system functioning, and those who remained made less money for the same work.

Not only was digital technology shrinking profit margins, but it was also rendering traditional bankers obsolete in many ways. Just as many music fans discovered that an Internet connection eliminated the need for shopping in bricks-and-mortar record stores, and the MP3 file meant they no longer needed to buy plastic discs, and just as many travelers discovered that they didn't need a travel agent when they could book plane tickets and hotel rooms online, many customers for financial products found that they could save money by cutting out the middle man: the stockbroker, personal banker, loan officer, or insurance agent.

The Internet was also doing to banks what it was doing to newspapers: it put banks all over the country in competition with one another, as potential customers could go online to compare interest rates on loans or credit cards and then apply for them far more quickly and easily than in the past. In these and other ways, digital technology was crushing the profitability of each traditional loan. Bankers were facing a career crisis familiar to many people in the digital age: forced to consider getting a new job. Millions in the United States and around the world face similar threats and disruptions, but bankers perhaps more than those in any other profession had the ability to use their influence with government to avoid those changes. Instead of adapting themselves to the new technologies that could bring greater price integrity and visibility to their industry, they coupled some of those technologies with their influence over government to reduce visibility, price integrity, and choice, and thereby secure higher profits for banks. Specifically, financial innovators created a new kind of digital bond.

The Magic Money Blender

These new blended bonds, called consolidated debt obligations, or CDOs, appeared to hold great promise. CDOs seemed to be the best solution ever found to an essential problem that makes banking necessary but that traditional banking had solved only partway: the problem of trapped capital. Remember that in the story of the original Levittown, consumers wanted to buy houses and builders wanted to build them, but the builders didn't have enough capital to build and the buyers didn't have enough capital to buy. Both buyers and builders expected to make money, but it was trapped in the future. Banks, with guarantees from the government, provided the capital, allowing the game to begin. But traditional mortgages went only so far in freeing capital for productive uses. The main drawback of the traditional banking system was its slowness. If you were a traditional banker who made your money by selling typical mortgages, thirty years was a long time to wait to get all your money back and loan it out again. Traditional loans improved the amount of available money, but they left local banks short on cash.

One solution was mortgage bonds. After a bank authorized a

$1 million loan, it didn't have to wait thirty years for all the money to come back. Instead an investment bank would buy the right to receive those payments when they came in and give the original bank that loaned the $1 million less money—say, $800,000—immediately. This mortgage bond was just a loan of a loan: the local bank gives the home buyer money today in return for a greater payment over time, and the investment bank gives the local bank money today in return for those same payments expected over time. The investment bank makes the same bet about the local bank that the local bank made about the individual borrower: that the loan, now called a mortgage bond, will be paid back.

But while mortgages addressed the immediate desire for money for home buyers, and mortgage bonds addressed the immediate desire for money at the local banks that sold mortgages, the investment banks and their clients were still left waiting thirty years for their payments to come in. The newfangled CDOs gave banks a way to sell investors bets on whether all of us will be able to pay all our bills. All the capital that was trapped in loans and other obligations could now be sold immediately. No one had to wait. In theory, this meant that every worthwhile transaction possible today—every business loan, every house purchase—could go forward, as it would not be held up for insufficient funds. The hope was that the economy would now run like a perfectly oiled engine, and that with such amazing computer-age oil, there would be no friction at all. This was the amazing promise of the supercharged economy invented by Rubin, Clinton, Greenspan, Summers, Gramm, and their colleagues.

If you buy a mortgage bond, you own a share in the house payments that borrowers expect to pay back in the future. Another type of bond, called an asset-backed security, is exactly like a mortgage loan except that instead of owning the right to collect money for the repayment of homes loans, you've bought the right to collect on credit cards, car loans, and other debt payments. Because computers could track seemingly infinite amounts of data, they made it possible to take these existing bonds and supersize them into CDO monster bonds. Computers would now allow an investor to buy into any kind of payments expected in the future: boat loans, college loans, gym memberships, and any other commitments to sending money on a regular schedule. The new idea in banking was to take every kind of obligation to repay borrowed money—trillions of dollars' worth— put them into a statistical blender, and then sell portions of the mixture as investments.

Monster Bonds Explode

Investment banks wanted to sell this new kind of bond to the wealthiest buyers: among them, the state pension managers who controlled investment and retirement money. But in order to protect people's life savings, the law states that pension funds for teachers, police, and many others can be invested only in bonds that receive the highest rating—AAA—from one of the government-approved ratings agencies such as Standard & Poor's. There are other factors in this calculation, but central to getting the AAA rating is the overall average credit rating of each person whose debt is held in the blended bonds. The computer models were designed with the expectation that most of the loans blended to create the new bond had been well vetted by the banks involved, and that the likelihood of getting paid back was about average. But investment banks started intentionally mixing low-risk loans, such as credit cards of wealthy people, with high-risk loans, such as housing loans to poor folks with a dicier chance of meeting their obligations. The mix of high- and low-risk loans produced the same credit score as a mix of more medium-risk loans, but the safe loans in the blender didn't provide any protection to the seriously risky ones. It was a classic instance of making cheap candy bars with rocks inside.

This deceptive blending is what the Securities and Exchange Commission (SEC) accused Goldman Sachs of doing in a 2010 lawsuit. As reported by the *Financial Times,* John Paulson of the hedge fund Paulson & Co. presented Goldman with a list of 123 securities backed by mortgages in California, Arizona, Nevada, and Florida. What those mortgages had in common was that "house prices were overheated and . . . mortgage defaults were going to rise." Goldman created a blended CDO monster bond out of these funds that were expected to fail, calling it Abacus. The blend was engineered to qualify for a AAA rating. So while Goldman sold shares of Abacus to investors who lacked the visibility to understand it was of poor quality, Paulson was buying credit insurance from the giant corporation American International Group—better known as AIG—against the bond's failure. When the securities underlying Abacus failed, according to the SEC complaint, its investors lost over $1 billion, while Paulson made $1 billion in profit, collecting insurance money from AIG that taxpayers paid in the form of the bailout. Goldman Sachs, meanwhile, kept around $25 million in fees.

Why on earth would we allow hardworking Americans' retirement savings to be invested in high-risk credit that was falsely rated AAA? Heck, investors and pension managers were *happy* to buy CDOs in the short term because they promised such high returns. Governors all over the country liked these bonds because the extra high returns made it seem like they could expect much higher returns for their states' pensions than they would see otherwise. In addition, it created the illusion that they had more money in their budgets, which freed them to spend money on their constituents and improve their chances of reelection. Politicians at *every* level were happy because the bankers getting rich selling these bonds kept making political donations. And ordinary citizens found that they could get cheap mortgages and easy credit cards; this was the beginning of preapproved credit card applications appearing in every mailbox and car loans offering 0 percent financing—that is, interest-free. There was no constituency to protest that the banks were luring pensions into purchasing toxic bonds. We were too busy enjoying our new houses, cars, and wide-screen TVs, all bought with cheap credit.

Monster bonds promised to be the lucrative new product that bankers could sell to replace the income they had lost to technological advances. But the risks for CDO sellers were big. What if the borrowers who made up the original loans repackaged as securities couldn't make their payments? Where would that leave the banks that had bundled loans together and issued them as CDOs?

To protect themselves, the banks created a marketplace where they could buy insurance policies against defaulting on these CDO monster bonds. They didn't call it insurance, however, as insurance is carefully regulated by the government to make sure that insurers hold on to enough money to pay claims against them. In other words, traditional insurance, like traditional lending, had capital requirements. To get around this obstacle, the investment banks called their insurance derivatives, or credit default swaps. Originally, these "swaps" were designed for businesses that depended on commodities that had volatile prices. Imagine that you sold heating oil to residential customers. If the price shot up too quickly, some customers on fixed incomes, such as pensioners, might not be able to afford to heat their homes. Buying into the derivatives market allowed you to buy a kind of insurance policy: if the price shot up, you would receive a payment on your insurance policy and that money would offset your increased costs. You had effectively swapped responsibility for a price rise with someone else and you could now offer your customers a more consistent price over time. That meant you would lose fewer customers to fluctuations in price.

But once a "swaps" market had been created, outsiders could buy in, too. These outsiders were like bettors at a race track: they were not running in the race, they were only looking for an opportunity to gamble. Banks and other companies began to "swap" responsibility for defaults on the loans they had bundled into CDOs. It was less like traditional insurance and more like a betting parlor: companies and banks would place bets about which banks would default on these new forms of bundled loans. The derivatives or "swaps" market mixed both kinds of buyers—those using the market to even out their business costs and those looking for someplace to gamble.

The credit insurance was and still is bought and sold in a private market, so no one had the legal right to see how many deals were being done or at what price. The same debt was frequently insured, insured, and insured again, and each time banks collected commissions. This new low-visibility, high-commission business replaced the commissions lost when the digital age took the easy money out of selling stocks and bonds. In many cases, bankers simply had to print and fill in the blanks on credit insurance forms.

The Magic Laws

How was this possible? Because banksters had used their political influence to change the rules that had governed banking and insurance. The Financial Services Modernization Act of 1999, sponsored by Republican Representatives Phil Gramm of Texas, Jim Leach of Iowa, and Thomas Bliley of Virginia, revoked the rule, established after the stock market crash of 1929, that no one company could act as a traditional bank, a Wall Street investment firm, and an insurance company at the same time. Now a single bank could take your money for safekeeping and use it as collateral to fund investments in high-risk securities with no supervision, all the while insuring itself against losses that taxpayers must pay if the bets the banks made with our money went bad.

In 2000 the Commodity Futures Modernization Act officially deregulated the derivatives market. Sponsored by Senator Richard Lugar, Republican of Indiana, and cosponsored by Senator Tom Harkin, Democrat of Iowa, among others, the new law stated that because derivatives were deals between "sophisticated parties" presumed to know what they were getting into, they did not need any oversight at all. In the *Frontline* episode "The Warning," which aired on October 20, 2009, Michael Greenberger, former director of the Commodity Futures Trade Commission, explained, "Now this is an unregulated market: no transparency, no capital reserve requirements, no prohibition on fraud, no prohibition on manipulation, no regulation of intermediaries. All the fundamental templates that we learned from the Great Depression that are needed to have markets function smoothly are gone."

The new laws and system produced an ever-expanding game

of risk transfer—essentially, playing hot potato with debt. With no rules for capital requirements to hold back anyone, every loan of every kind now represented a chance for banksters to profit by selling insurance on something so big that they would never have to pay claims on it. By removing capital requirements—the traditional incentive for banks to act as price integrity police—the standard of making careful, educated investments was replaced by the incentive to sell as much insurance on as much debt as possible.

The old alignment of interests—that banks and their customers all wanted everyone in the country to pay their debts—was replaced by its opposite. As in the case of Abacus, banks could actually make more money from bonds that defaulted than from those that were paid. It was analogous to a carmaker's deciding that instead of striving to sell you safe, reliable cars, it will build cheap, faulty cars likely to explode—and then insure them against explosion. When your car blows up in that scenario, the car company keeps both the price you paid for the car *and* the settlement money from the insurance company. Selling exploding cars pays better than selling good ones. In an unregulated market, where no VICI code ensures that cars offered for sale are safe, it's the most profitable choice—as long as you're not the car buyer or a passenger in the wreck.

Cheating was no longer a side game, it was the primary game—not because people suddenly became greedier but because their interests were no longer aligned. The incentives now rewarded theft. The new rules, or rather the new lack of rules, rewarded secrecy instead of visibility, misinformation over price integrity, stealing from clients instead of serving them, quantity over quality, and short-term revenue over long-term value. Ordinary Americans' savings, instead of being directed into productive investments that could grow the

Banking

Every choice to align the interests of bankers with everyone else through capital requirements enhances productive investment; every choice to breach it destroys it.

Where does the money go?

Tax Code
Tax code rewards speculators and extractors, punishes savers, investors, and inventors, adding more fuel for the game.

Capital Requirements
In the year 2000, the creation of swaps markets effectively eliminates capital requirements for almost all lending. This reverses traditional incentives for investment leading to rampant credit speculation and creates a $600 trillion gambling parlor: the bigger the bets, the bigger the winnings.

Ratings Agencies
The rating agencies, paid by the companies they're meant to supervise, hand out AAA ratings to keep the game going.

Short-Term Results
• Easy credit
• Kick the Can politics
• Massive debt
• Declining investment
• Incentive to create debt not value

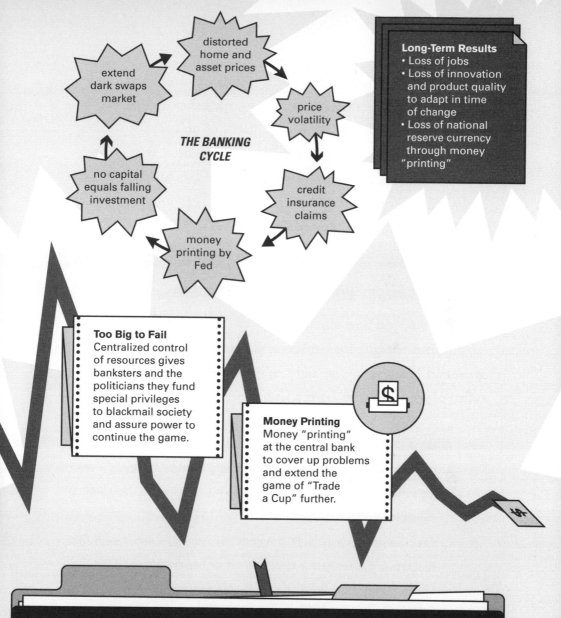

distorted home and asset prices

extend dark swaps market

price volatility

THE BANKING CYCLE

no capital equals falling investment

credit insurance claims

money printing by Fed

Long-Term Results
- Loss of jobs
- Loss of innovation and product quality to adapt in time of change
- Loss of national reserve currency through money "printing"

Too Big to Fail
Centralized control of resources gives banksters and the politicians they fund special privileges to blackmail society and assure power to continue the game.

Money Printing
Money "printing" at the central bank to cover up problems and extend the game of "Trade a Cup" further.

THE FIX

How to "Reset" the Game without a major war.

1 Mandate capital requirements throughout entire lending system.

2 End conflict of interest. Ban banks from paying for ratings.

3 Reverse tax code to incentivize investment and punish speculation and extraction.

4 Impose capital requirements to force banks to restructure to reduce global risk.

5 "Cancel" debt instead of "printing" money.

economy for the future, were being funneled directly to the big banks and their credit casino, which awarded their top people bonuses totaling in the hundreds of millions of dollars. For stealing! The traditional banking industry had become undead, feeding on its customers and on the taxpayers who guaranteed its bad deals. Banking, which had once served the economy, had become a vampire extracting the lifeblood of American capitalism.

Capitalism Versus Extractionism

To show just how important it is to our economy that we have capital requirements for bankers and insurers, I created two little games I'd like you to play right now in your imagination. They're called Make a Cup and Trade a Cup.

MAKE A CUP RULES

1. Each player in the game is a Banker trying to make money by investing money in Cup Makers, who produce the one product that matters: cups that are used by Customers.

2. Each Banker is given limited amount of money to invest with Cup Makers. A Banker gets a return on his or her investment if the Cup Maker makes a great cup, one that creates value in some way, that is bigger, more beautiful, more efficiently produced than the cups that other Bankers are investing in.

3. The game continues as long as there are enough cups for all the Customers.

If you play this game, you will find that because Bankers have only a limited amount of money and have to compete with many other

Bankers and Cup Makers, it is in Bankers' interest to be very careful about choosing which Cup Makers to invest with. Over time, only the best Bankers who do the most research and spend the most time developing their investments will survive, and only the best Cup Makers will make it to market. Because there are so many Bankers and Cup Makers in the game, there is ongoing innovation—lots of new and different cups to choose from. The system is highly adaptable to change: no matter what sort of cup Customers want or need, some Bankers will fund some Cup Makers to create a cup that suits their needs.

The result is that the rules of Make a Cup create a system in which good Cup Makers get financing, society gets good cups, and Bankers' interests are aligned with those of their Customers. The outcome is widely shared, highly adaptable resources and a wide variety of interesting cups to suit all tastes and styles. Make a Cup is capitalism as it is intended to work, with the rules of the banking industry aligning the players' interests to create a productive, innovative, and prosperous society.

In contrast, Trade a Cup changes one rule of the game: now there are two kinds of Bankers, Traditional Bankers with limited access to money and Special Bankers who have unlimited access to money. But this one change turns capitalism into its exact opposite—extractionism.

TRADE A CUP RULES

1. Each player is either a Traditional Banker or a Special Banker. Both types of Banker begin by attempting to make money by investing in Cup Makers.

2. Traditional Bankers are given limited amounts of money to invest with Cup Makers, just as in Make a Cup, but Special Bankers can bor-

row as much money as they want from the players group bank. (It's as if they can take money from the Monopoly bank whenever they choose.) Like the banksters that sell credit insurance through swaps today, Special Bankers have no capital requirements limiting their borrowing and lending. They can invest with Cup Makers or make loans to other people to buy and sell or trade cups.

3. The game continues as long as there are enough cups for all the Customers.

When you play Trade a Cup, you will see that the Traditional Bankers still try to find and invest with good cup makers and make good cups. But when they find talented and efficient Cup Makers, they are outbid by the Special Bankers who have unlimited access to money. Soon, the Special Bankers will have launched a bidding war among themselves. The price of cups will be bid so high that the Traditional Bankers will run out of money. Many Customers will no longer be able to afford cups.

Special Bankers will then discover that the easiest way to make sure everyone still gets a cup (so the game can continue) is to buy all the cups and rent them back to Customers for a small fee. This will make their job much easier, because unlike Traditional Bankers, Special Bankers will no longer have to be as discriminating in their investments. When the Special Bankers control most of the cups and make their profits by trading cups among themselves and by renting them to customers, it doesn't matter if the cups are high quality or low. Customers will have to take whatever cups are available and affordable. Many Cup Makers will quit because when the money is being made trading and renting cups, any cup will do, and there is little reward for making better cups and it is very expensive to try.

But the Special Bankers who now own most of the cups will know that the price of cups is now artificially high from previous unlimited bidding. They will worry that cup prices might collapse (and they own most of the cups!). To solve the problem, the Special Bankers will offer to lower the cost of renting cups in exchange for the Customers selling insurance to Bankers on the value of all the cups. This gives all the players in the game a short-term incentive to agree to sell the Special Bankers the insurance and accept the risk that the value of all the cups in the game might collapse.

Now, Trade a Cup gets ugly. With all the cup prices so high, and the cup selection and quality so low, even the boldest of the Special Bankers knows that a cup that used to sell for $5 in the game and that now costs $500 simply isn't worth it. Market confidence will reach a tipping point, and cup prices will drop. The Special Bankers who own most of the cups will take enormous losses, triggering the insurance policies they bought from all the Customers.

If the Customers don't pay the Special Bankers the insurance money, the Special Bankers will threaten to withhold all the cups, which they now own. And even though the cups are expensive and poor quality, the game can't go on without them, so Customers will agree to pay the insurance on the Special Bankers' cup losses: poor quality, expensive cups are better than no cups at all.

By now, the number of available cups is at an all-time low, the cost of cups (to buy, not rent) is at an all-time high, and Customers are actually paying twice for every cup, once when they rent a cup and again when they pay the insurance claims on everybody's cups to the Special Bankers. There are few available jobs for Cup Makers. Customers may wish to stop paying insurance to the Special Bankers, but every time they threaten not to pay the insurance, all the Special Bankers have to do is threaten to take away access to cups. Sadly, this game can last a long time, as the Special Bankers continue extracting money from the economy. Where the old rules of Make a Cup produced a capitalist economy that was thriving and prosperous, the rule change that created Trade a Cup now makes the economy wither.

TRADE A CUP CAN END IN ONE OF THREE WAYS:

1. **Riot, Revolution, and War.** Some Customers become enraged and want to attack the Special Bankers who have been extracting their money. The game enters a period of violence until so many cups are broken that there are no longer enough to go around. Trade a Cup now becomes a terrible new game, Break a Cup, and everybody loses.

2. **Money Printing.** The players agree to "print" money from the central bank to pay off the Special Bankers' insurance claims and pay the rent on cups that increasing numbers of Customers can no longer afford. This defers rage and temporarily prevents riot, revolution, and war, though it lowers the value of the currency and undermines the economy even further.

3. **Reset Meeting.** All the players meet and acknowledge that the system has become dysfunctional. It is impossible to make cups anymore and there is a serious threat that the game will shift to Break a Cup. The Special Bankers agree to give up their "no capital requirements" status and to cancel a reasonable percentage of the debt they are trying to collect. Debt created in an environment without capital requirements (no real upfront costs) is simply not real. To make sure that no cups are broken during the transition back to capital requirements, the players agree to institute capital requirements gradually and predictably through every part of the game for the benefit of all

who are at risk if a cup breaks. With capital requirements, Trade a Cup naturally turns back into Make a Cup. The game can continue and the economy can prosper again.

The lesson in these games is simple. As long as Special Bankers have unlimited money to play in the game, interests will be misaligned, prices for cups will get distorted, the selection (choice) will diminish, and the quality will drop. Options one and two (violence and money printing) will seem attractive in the short run, but fail to stop the underlying extraction. That extraction will continue until the players achieve option three and restore capital requirements to realign their interests

Once all the Bankers and other players agree to attempt option three, the most delicate and important work will be managing Customers' rage at the unfairness of the game. Only if that rage is acknowledged and that energy is directed at the solution to the root problem can all the players escape the endless cycle of debt, unfairness and violence and return to prosperity.

Too Big to Fail

Back in reality, we are still stuck in our national game of Trade a Cup. We call our real-life special bankers SIFIs, or systematically important financial institutions—meaning that they are "too big to fail." Because if just one of those banks were to go under, it could trigger a cascade of failures that could threaten the entire system and cost every American his or her cup. And so we promise to bail them out no matter how expensive it gets.

In 2008, it was as if some business associates of yours knocked on your door one evening after a night in Vegas. You invite them in, and they tell you the sad story of their gambling losses, which they somehow expect you to cover. You refuse. Now imagine that your colleagues grab you, tie you up, and toss you into your bathtub. Then one of them turns on the taps. As water rises close to your face, another one offers you a deal: if you will cover all of their debts tonight, they will lend you a snorkel.

What do you think the government negotiator in the bathtub said to the banksters? I'll tell you. Under threat of continued financial decline and after dozens of programs worth billions of dollars failed to stop the financial markets from falling, Ben Bernanke, the chairman of the Federal Reserve, said repeatedly through the winter of 2009 that he would do whatever was "necessary" to "stabilize" the banking system—in effect, that there was no amount of money he would not provide to cover the banksters' losses. To their ears, as I heard in my interviews with the banking community, that meant infinite money: Trade a Cup goes on!

The cover-up has been so good that nothing has been done to change the extractionist loopholes created in 2000, allowing credit insurance to be sold in private markets with little capital requirements and forcing ratings agencies to depend on the banks whose bonds they rate for payment to remain intact. Not a single American political leader has even suggested capital requirements or debt cancelation, and few have made headway on the conflict of interest inherent in the current ratings system. No politician seems willing to introduce VICI into the corrupt ratings system.

The Expanding Ripples:
The Jobs, Housing, and Food Crises

The US central bank addressed the crisis of 2008 by becoming the "buyer of last resort" and buying up the toxic bonds that no one else would touch anymore. To pay for all of these purchases, the Fed began the policy of quantitative easing, a confusing term for what is essentially printing extra money out of thin air. The hope was that if it could prop up the system for a few years, then investment and jobs would return. The flaw in the Fed's theory was that little was done to realign the interests of the banks with the interests of their clients and the national economy. As a result, the more money the government pumped into the system, the more money the bankers extracted.

Before the system collapsed, a huge percentage of the money "created" by the Magic Money Machine went into real estate: bigger homes, summer homes, homes built as short-term investments to be "flipped," and equivalent commercial real estate purchases for companies. As home buyers received supersized loans, they used their extra cash to bid up housing prices. Vast numbers of buildings that wouldn't have been built otherwise were bought at prices no one would have paid only a few years before. In this way, the credit derivatives market helped inflate the real estate bubble of 2000–07. And when the financial crisis hit, millions of people found themselves locked into contracts to pay these hugely inflated housing prices.

Making matters worse, in the face of the financial crisis, the banks scaled back lending, so that businesses couldn't obtain the loans they expected: neither the short-term loans that businesses use to cover fluctuating costs nor the long-term loans that facilitate expansions and new ventures. Companies and investors that still had reserves of capital went on defense, investing in gold, oil, and other commodities. Businesses that depended on short-term loans to function could no longer borrow the money they needed, and their only choice was to lay off workers to cut costs. That created a ripple of higher unemployment, which meant that even fewer workers had enough income to make their inflated housing payments; which in turn forced the banks to take another hit as a new round of loan defaults began. In this way, "too big to fail" created the unemployment foreclosure and debt crisis of 2009–12. It was not the result of subprime lending and credit speculation—those first bad mortgages were cleared out of the market by early 2009, according to the *Washington Post*. At that time, most of the subprime loans had been worked out or were in foreclosure, and prime loans became the largest single slice of foreclosures, caused by the spike in unemployment.

The abstractions of the financial crisis hit home in ways that any working person can understand: lost jobs, lost homes, lost retirement savings, and lost hope. Beyond the $12,000 share of the increased national debt assumed by each American, there were additional, even more serious costs. First was the unfairness of ordinary Americans paying a hidden tax, while the banksters were bailed out one hundred cents on the dollar. As Representative Alan Grayson of Florida remarked to me, "It turns out crime does pay."

Next came the government's attempts to hide the costs of the bailout by printing extra money. As hedge fund manager Bill Fleckenstein explained on my show, doing this has its own ripple effect. The lucky banks that received this free money had to put it somewhere, and now that the real estate market no longer seemed safe, they bought commodities, driving up the price of gold and oil and food. Few of us need gold, but everyone needs energy and food, and so the pain of the bankers' bailout spread. In 2010 alone, according to the Oliver Wyman management consulting firm, the price of coffee rose 77 percent; wheat, 47 percent; and cotton for clothes, 84 percent. Instead of a real estate bubble, the bailout created a global food and clothing bubble. For the middle class, that's a nuisance. For the poorest billion people in the world—and that includes the poorest Americans—who were already spending 70 percent of their disposable income on food, it's a disaster. They can no longer afford staples such as tortillas, rice, pasta, and couscous. The bank bailout and the government's attempt to cover up the massive banking theft create global misery.

In the long term, there is an even higher price to pay. All of the money diverted into insurance fraud and reckless speculation is not going into productive investments that could solve our problems. Many investors find that it's not worth the time, work, and patience to develop real products such as clean energy, improved health care, and so on when they can make money so much more easily by cheating. And small investors follow in the wake of big ones: how many people do you know who are putting their own extra money into the most promising green energy technologies? And how many do you know who are buying oil and gold? This is the most disastrous long-term consequence of Trade a Cup: not only do prices inflate but also productive work suffers because it doesn't pay as well as extraction. The smartest, most talented people discover that the big rewards go to special bankers. Who, then, wants to be a cup maker?

The damage to our economy and our shared future is far greater than the $12,000 of debt it imposed on each of us for the bailout. The true cost is incalculable and ongoing. Imagine that we went out together and ate an overpriced meal that turned out to be poisonous. By the end of the night, the price we paid for the meal would be the least of our concerns. That's the Very Bad Deal.

Aren't We Better Off Now?

You might assume that as costly as the bank bailout was, it preserved something of value. But as *Naked Capitalism* blogger Yves Smith (in the nonvirtual world, management consultant Susan Webber) told me, if we were to tax the largest banks for the cost of the global financial crisis over twenty years *it would cost over $1.5 trillion a year.* That's more than the market capitalization of the biggest banks of the world. So banks are, in her words, "net value destroyers": it's not just that bank bailouts have been incredibly expensive but also that banks actually cost taxpayers more than they are worth. Their only benefit is to the economy as a whole—but that is the benefit that has been destroyed since the 1990s. This is the mathematical definition of extraction.

Some people will tell you that the government had no choice but to stabilize the financial system. They'll tell you that some bailout money has been paid back, that the lessons have been learned, and that we will be safer in the future. That might be one-third true. Many banks and other companies that received money are paying it back—though none of them is repaying the greater losses we all suffered from the money printing that degrades our currency and costs us so much in jobs, houses, savings, and commodities.

It's true that lessons have been learned. Testifying before Congress on October 23, 2008, Alan Greenspan was asked by Representative Henry Waxman of California, "You have been a staunch advocate for letting markets regulate themselves. And my question for you is simple: Were you wrong?"

Greenspan answered, "Yes."

Larry Summers now says that he supports strong regulation of derivatives.

President Clinton told ABC News that when it came to deregulating financial markets in 1999 and 2000, "I think [Treasury secretaries Robert Rubin and Larry Summers] were wrong, and I think I was wrong to take" their advice.

After the financial crisis, a bipartisan commission of US senators issued the *Levin-Coburn Report*, which found that "the crisis was not a natural disaster, but the result of high-risk, complex financial products; undisclosed conflicts of interest; and the failure of regulators, the credit rating agencies, and the market itself to rein in the excesses of Wall Street."

The financial markets need regulation the way a nuclear power plant needs a cooling agent for its radioactive fuel rods. In a nuclear plant, if safety rules are enforced and the heat of the rods is properly controlled by a cooling agent, the result can be clean, abundant electricity. But if that cooling process is neglected , the fuel rods overheat and may cause a nuclear meltdown. Similarly, capital requirements are the cooling agent of risk taking in the economy, whether the risks are being taken by banks, consumers, or industry. Just as nuclear fuel will always be reactive, people will always be greedy. We need to enforce rules to balance natural greed with capital requirements so that greed can create productive risk taking and competition and not short-term extraction, otherwise known as theft.

How to Fix Banking

1. PUT "SWAPS" ON PUBLIC EXCHANGES

In Vegas, you need to have actual money to gamble—your own money—and if you lose, you pay. But since 2000, banks, industry, and consumers have been free to take on system-threatening levels of debt (to the point of financial meltdown) without facing any requirement to risk a significant amount of their own money. And while consumer risk taking was curbed by the 2008 financial crisis, US banks continue to use America's deposits insured by the Federal Deposit Insurance Corporation (FDIC) to fund their mad, bonus-seeking speculation. Once the banks blow through that, they borrow from the biggest money-printing house in the world, the US Federal Reserve. No one else in the world can pay themselves billions to take enormous risk with little or no money down.

To end this insanity the American people must demand an end to the anachronistic "dark market" for credit insurance, or swaps, and insist that they be moved to an exchange where the risks that we all now bear can be visible to all. (You might think Treasury Secretary Tim Geithner, after his experiences during the crisis, would have led the charge to restrict or ban risky swaps, especially after the Obama administration passed a bill that began to regulate these instruments. But one of Geithner's first decisions in using this new law was to exempt foreign currency swaps from the new regulations.) All trades on a theoretical swaps exchange must be required to meet capital requirements (or some equivalent inhibitor of risk) to stop the game of Trade a Cup for good.

Perhaps as important as the VICI integrity of capital requirements is the visibility that an exchange would create: we could all see who was trading and insuring what. One of the greatest obstacles in resolving the financial crisis in 2008 was the need to pay all the $600 trillion in swaps because central bankers couldn't see which swaps were legitimate insurance for energy and commodities—insurance that was essential to the smooth functioning of the economy—and which were idle speculation. Because the central bankers couldn't see the difference, they were forced to pay off everybody, including the reckless speculators. The same thing happened in the European bond market in 2011.

Home lending also needs additional capital requirements in the direct home lending and consumer credit markets for both private banks and government banks such as the Federal National Mortgage Association, commonly known as Fannie Mae, and the Federal Home Loan Mortgage Corporation, known as Freddie Mac. Every loan must require a down payment. All lenders must be at risk for losses from their loans. Only by keeping a portion of the risk from the loans they make will banks' interests remain aligned with the interests of their customers.

2. CANCEL SPECULATIVE DEBT—AND CLAW BACK BONUSES

Some of the promises that were made in the days of reckless gambling and irresponsible reliance on taxpayer money can't be kept. But as Mohammed El-Erian, CEO of the investment firm Pimco, told me, "The question is, how do you share that burden? So far the burden has been felt mainly by the real economy and households." Ordinary Americans have paid for bankers' mistakes. But while US home owners are under siege by creditor predator banks, and millions of unemployed debt holders are forced into a *Survivor*-like fight with one another over scraps, bondholders have been paid a hundred cents on the dollar with newly printed money. Banks have been bailed out with printed money. The real sacrifices have all been made by ordinary people in the forms of increased public debt, reduced pension payments, and reduced health benefits.

We must require not only that banks retain more capital but also that when they place bad bets, they pay the price for their losing bets themselves. Otherwise we are stuck with the worst of two economic systems: like a capitalist country, we have private banks that keep their profits. But like a communist country, we have a system where banking losses are charged to the government. Only when we end this corporate communism will we realign the interests of the banks with the investors they serve. The way to do this is debt reduction or cancelation. If the system is so out of control that we can use a computer to fabricate trillions in new money by simply adding some zeros, then surely we can find a way to delete some zeros as well. By definition, if you can print it, you can cancel it.

As we have already seen, a swap can either be an insurance policy that helps to lower long-term costs for a business or a bet by an outsider on whether a given company or country will succeed or fail. Putting swaps on a public exchange would create the visibility for all to see the difference between commodity insurance that is critical to the economy and speculative bets that are not much different from gambling. In fact, Richard Grasso, former chairman of the New York Stock Exchange, suggested to me in a personal interview that the speculative bets that fueled the financial crisis could be reclassified legally as online gaming—and then cancelled. His technical explanation: "I believe regulators should require the product to be registered with a central clearing agent (like an exchange) and thus able to be monitored globally to prevent contracts being written in excess of the debt obligations they are designed to insure (corporate or sovereign). This is easily accomplished by [regulators] and Treasury issuing a cross-markets rule adopted by non-US counterparts. Any contracts written outside these requirements would be deemed null and void by regulators as simply online gaming."

Similarly, bonuses collected by CEOs and board members of AAA-rated financial institutions on the basis of profits from reckless speculation should be "clawed back" and repaid. These leaders were the custodians for their institutions, with the responsibility to determine how much risk was safe to take. They should not keep bonus pay for losses caused by their own bad decisions just because those losses were covered by the government—that is, by ordinary taxpayers. The threat of future clawbacks will keep their personal interests aligned with the financial interests of their institutions and their country.

3. REVISE THE TAX CODE TO ENCOURAGE LONG-TERM INVESTMENT, NOT SHORT-TERM EXTRACTION

It seems to me that if we agree that there's nothing morally wrong with getting rich or being poor and that we want people to use their wealth in ways that increase productivity, then that's what our tax code should encourage. Maybe we should tax spending—consumption—rather than income, and let the tax code discourage short-term investors and reward long-term investors. If you find a way to use your computer to extract money from the stock market in a few seconds, you should be taxed very high. If you commit your money for years and launch a business and build something new that others can use, you should be taxed low. A well-run country is like any well-run business: greedy, but long-term greedy. We need a tax code that will bring out the "long-term greedy" in every American.

4. DON'T LET WALL STREET BUY THE RULES

The basic secrets of the derivatives market are now known, but the crisis was not caused simply by a failure of understanding. It was caused by a failure of our political system. In 2009 alone, banks spent $220 million lobbying against new regulations such as capital requirements and lobbying in favor of spending cuts to get budget deficits under control. But as Simon Johnson has written, "[The banks'] rhetoric is misleading at best. At worst it represents a blatant attempt to shake down the public purse." When the political conversation turns to debt, it usually hides the reasons we ran up this debt and the fundamental culpability of the greedy bastards on Wall Street.

When Wall Street isn't buying access to our legislators, they are buying the very ratings agencies relied on by pension managers to evaluate how risky a given investment is. Wall Street banks pay Standard & Poor's and Moody's to rate their bonds. The better the rating, the more the banks can sell, and the more money ratings agencies and banks make. But considering the massive risks given to the world's pension and insurance managers by Wall Street and the ratings agencies, shouldn't the risk evaluation be paid for by the group buying the investment—not selling it?

5. HOLD AN INTERNATIONAL RESET MEETING

Historically, debt reset meetings have come after global conflicts such as World War II and the American Civil War. In these meetings, governments realigned the interests of countries and financial institutions using tools such as infrastructure banks (which provide temporary lending when private institutions no longer can), tax reforms, debt cancelations, and new banking regulations. Given our previous hellish experiences with large-scale war, however, I suspect that many of us would prefer to fix the problem first and skip the war. We cannot allow giant creditors to turn fights over debt into currency wars and then into real wars. Our opportunity in this generation is to resolve the global debt imbalance with a new Marshall Plan before a war begins.

3

International Trading Pirates

In 1791, US Secretary of the Treasury Alexander Hamilton presented his *Report on Manufactures* to the recently formed US Congress. Hamilton understood the importance of manufacturing because he saw how the British army was well supplied during the Revolutionary War, while his own army lacked for ammunition, boots, and winter coats. He intended never to allow his country to be so vulnerable again. From 1789 to 1993, America had a dedicated

policy of manufacturing essential goods and services on its own, or ensuring that multinationals that made critical goods operated in alignment with US interests.

But from 1993 onward, American corporate elites cut a deal with Chinese elites to wreck this well-honed system. We can see the effects of this bad deal by following "American" goods back to their source. General Electric has made lightbulbs since the days of Thomas Edison, but in 2007, GE decided to begin outsourcing its next generation of bulbs to China. GE will profit from licensing its patents and marketing the products, while leaving the physical production to the Chinese. Similarly, American car company General Motors now sells more cars in China than in the United States, according to *Money* magazine. GM has closed thirteen US plants since it filed for bankruptcy in 2009, but it has opened fifteen plants in China in the last ten years.

An ever-increasing list of essential products is now manufactured abroad rather than at home. "It's not just shoes and textiles and furniture that are now exclusively made offshore," wrote Steven Pearlstein, the business and economics columnist for the *Washington Post*, "it's also high-tech products that were invented here. Think of computer chips, smartphones, solar cells, and wind turbines. And now . . . research and development is beginning to move offshore as well."

Where Did the Good Jobs Go?

Our economy used to be based on making things ourselves, which provided jobs for Americans as well as consumer goods. But more and more, we consume products that are made, packaged, and assembled abroad, which means that the jobs have gone abroad, too—most notably to China. According to the *Wall Street Journal*, most people who lost jobs in the recent recession found new ones, but at lower pay. In fact, over one-third of those lucky enough to find new employment had to accept pay cuts of at least 20 percent.

Pay cuts? We haven't experienced real, sustained pay cuts since the 1930s. We all know that the 2008–09 recession was terrible, but what is unusual is that the recovery has been terrible too. Only certain segments of the economy improved. Seemingly, productivity increased. Profits increased. The stock market recovered. Corporate profits rose, giving corporations extra money for investing. Interest rates remained at historic lows, so it was cheaper than ever to borrow money to invest. But the job market and domestic investment market didn't recover. All that corporate cash had to go somewhere. Why wasn't it going into new ventures, and research and development, and expanding existing businesses, creating a surge in new jobs?

We know that a lot of money is being sucked into the banking casinos, but certainly not all of it. Where was all that free trade money?

The simple answer is that the money had already been divvied up. Part of it is going to finance manufacturing in China and part of it is staying here with our bankers and the superrich. Big industry—companies such as Caterpillar, General Electric, John Deere, Cummins Engine, and automakers, among others—was investing far more in China than here. American banks (which we subsidize!) were increasing their lending to China rather than lending capital here. Andrew Liveris, CEO of the Dow Chemical Company, put it bluntly: "US companies—run by patriotic people—are moving off-shore at the fastest rate in history."

The fact is, if you and I had a spare $100 million to invest, we'd be tempted to send it to China too. It's so much easier to make money investing in that country's short-term growth at our long-term expense, whether you're a major corporation, a private investor, or a bank. But why should it be? Why?

The reason why is because of government policy. Our current, highly regulated trading arrangements benefit international investors who want to profit from sending capital to low-wage countries such as China. You can read the evidence yourself. In December 2005, a little-known but extremely powerful group of American economic policy makers met in what's called the Federal Open Market Committee (FOMC) meeting. The FOMC is the policy-making body of the Federal Reserve; the people around that table decide whether to lower or raise interest rates, monitor instability in the financial system (or bury their heads in the sand; whatever the case may be), and discuss various regions of America and their economic performances. You might have glimpsed the power of this group if you've ever watched the stock market go crazy after the Fed has moved to bail out the world economy (or not).

One of the men in the room at the time, Dallas Fed president Richard Fisher, had a complaint about China. As revealed in the minutes of the December 2005 meeting, Fisher was bitter about the enormous quantity of Chinese goods flowing into America. He pointed out that this was creating "disinflation," or lowering prices and wages for Americans, and that the CEOs he was talking to were frustrated about the tide of goods and services coming into the country. Except that Fisher wasn't griping that there were too many Chinese imports; he was angry that there *weren't enough* imports! Even though China had built special export-only ports for shipping goods out of China, the American ports can't absorb what China wants to sell us because of what he called "work rules"—in other words, unions, being "slow to adjust." This presented a huge problem, Fisher continued, because it was blocking his CEO contacts from outsourcing as much work abroad as quickly as possible. In his words, they were not "exploiting globalization" fast enough.

Disturbingly, in that same meeting, Fisher *bragged* about the weakness, at that time, of Ford: "My most delicious irony is the fact that similarly dated Vietnamese debt now trades on a price basis richer, and on a yield basis lower, than that of Ford Motor Company." In other words, a developing Asian country was financially stronger, as measured by the value of its debt, than one of the most significant employers in the United States. The response from his fellow banksters? Laughter.

Why would the Dallas Federal Reserve Bank president celebrate the strength of Chinese exports and Vietnamese debt? Simple: moving work to China weakens American workers. When you can't find a job, or your only choice is to accept a pay cut or face layoffs, you're much less likely to strike. That means multinational corporations benefit twice when they move manufacturing to China. Not only do they get to pay Chinese workers extremely low wages but they also build the leverage to lower wages and limit the rights of their US employees.

Now, you might consider this is an outrage. And you might wonder why it wasn't reported widely in 2005 that a powerful economic player like Richard Fisher was openly arguing for shipping the US manufacturing base to China faster than it was already happening, at the urging of corporate CEOs in Texas. Are you sitting down? The reason it wasn't reported at the time is that transcripts of FOMC meetings are kept secret for five years. (And that five-year lag is an *improvement*—it used to be that the meetings were secret and the transcripts shredded.) This transcript was released only in 2010, while the world financial system was melting down. So very few read it, let alone reported on it. Besides, five years later, it's old news, right? So why would any journalist report it as significant?

But it *is* significant. The US national strategy is and has been, for many years now, to move as much production to China as quickly as possible. It is stated outright by powerful policy makers, not when and where the public is paying attention. This is the strategy of CEOs and political decision makers like Richard Fisher: promote disastrous policies that are misaligned with the interests of hardworking Americans. Just make sure to do it from behind closed doors.

Before I go on to describe the basics of our trading relationship, and why it is a destructive, short-term, greedy model, you should recognize that just by knowing what the people who set these policies believe, you have weakened their power. What I am about to describe is upsetting, but remember, you can solve only what you have the courage to see. By learning, you are helping America to begin to conduct itself differently.

So hang on, and keep reading.

How to Screw Your Trading Partner

China's strategy is called mercantilism, which means that interest groups within one country rig their own currency and tax code to lure foreign investment away from other countries. It's a deliberate breach of price integrity to change the flow of money and opportunity, and many countries have done it.

Between 1992 and 1994 China devalued its currency, known as the yuan or renminbi, by about 60 percent. (Many smaller Asian countries followed.) With Chinese currency costing half of what it had before, it was as if the entire nation of China were on sale at 60 percent off! American-made products looked more than twice as expensive the world over. Following the devaluation, a flood of foreign investments (including some from massive American corporations and banks) and jobs arrived in China.

In the same period, China was negotiating with the United States to win most favored nation status, meaning that the United States would trade with China on the best possible terms. Traditionally, that status was reserved for countries with whom our trading relationships advanced American interests—or at least didn't threaten them. This was the goal so important to Alexander Hamilton. For instance, while the United States traded with the Soviet Union during the Cold War, our government carefully managed the process so that the Soviets could not gain technology they could use against us. But in a massive break with historical precedent, we granted China MFN status in 1999 and made it permanent in 2000. Now not only were there huge tax and currency advantages to building factories in China rather than in America, but US companies that did so could be assured of excellent treatment once they got there. In the next ten years, the US trade deficit with China grew from 83 billion dollars in 2000 to 273 billion dollars.

Tax Games

These policies brought about a huge, unnatural price disparity between the United States and China. One reason that it's so much more profitable for investors to make money in China is tariffs, or the taxes that countries charge on imports. When you or I buy something made in China, our government taxes that import at the rate of 2.5 percent. But when a Chinese person buys something made in the USA, his government taxes it at 25 percent—ten times the tax. As a result, many Chinese people find they get a better deal buying domestic products than American goods. But it's also more profitable to start a company in China and sell to America, where tariffs are low, than to start a company in America and sell to China, where tariffs are high. For that one reason, investors know that they will make more money investing in similar companies over there than here. So US investors send their money to China, stoking Chinese growth and creating jobs in the Chinese economy rather than at home.

Now we can see what happened to US jobs. We used to make clothes here; now they are made largely in China. We used to make auto parts and computer batteries here; now more and more are made in China. We used to make *American flags* here; now more are made in China. And so on and so forth. American CEOs just can't exploit China fast enough. In 2000, according to the US Bureau of Labor Statistics, about 17.1 million people worked in manufacturing; as of July 2011, the figure was 11.7 million. The Chinese manufacturing sector grew enormously in comparison to America's. That was not, as some claim, because increase American productivity meant we needed fewer workers. As Ian Fletcher, a senior economist at the Coalition for a Prosperous America, wrote in the Huffington Post: "There is no way this can be attributed to a sudden surge of productivity, as there simply aren't any manufacturing innovations that suddenly came online in 2000. . . . We've had productivity growth in manufacturing for 200 years without seeing a sudden drop like that." The change came because China pursued one of the most protectionist policies ever seen from a modern state, launching history's biggest trade war—and winning.

And we let them. "Americans acquiesced to this off-shoring because it fattened corporate profits, lowered consumer prices, and fit neatly with a free-trade-free-market consensus among the economic elite," wrote Steven Pearlstein in the *Washington Post*. Corporations were happy, at least in the short term, making easy money. Consumers got everyday low prices at Wal-Mart. As jobs and earnings dwindled at home, we drove to our big box stores to get our Chinese-made bargains. And politicians liked the one-size-fits-all economic policy: Just say "the free market," and—Abracadabra!—everything seemed to be okay. The Very Bad Deal candy bar tasted great, and it took a while before we bit down on the rock.

How to Make a Pirate

Not only were enormous numbers of good American jobs getting moved overseas, and not only was US wealth being drained to build up our biggest economic rival, but something disturbing and far less widely known was happening: American companies were losing their allegiance to the United States. As former California congressman Rep. Duncan L. Hunter said in an interview with *Manufacturing News*, "for practical purposes, many of the multinational corporations have become Chinese corporations. They like the fact that they are subsidized by their new government, which is China, and that they're able to push American products that are made in the United States off the shelves."

Wal-Mart, to give one example, became increasingly a Chinese company, orchestrating the shipment of goods made by poor Chinese workers to increasingly poor American workers. According to a report by labor research group Global Labor Strategies, "If the US retail giant Wal-Mart were a country, it would be China's eighth-largest trading partner." The report continues, "Roughly 66% of the increase in Chinese exports in the past 12 years can be attributed to non-Chinese-owned global companies and their joint ventures. Foreign-owned global corporations account for 60% of Chinese exports to the US." Recently, GM president Tim Lee spoke enthusiastically to the *Wall Street Journal* about company efforts to "look at every export potential out of China." His comments led my friend Dan DiMicco, CEO of the steel manufacturer Nucor Corp., to ask me, "Just how long do you think it will be before GM cars *made in China* will be flooding our shores?" It's not just that Chinese companies are taking our money and our jobs. It's that American companies are making a killing by *acting like Chinese companies themselves*. They are responding to a Chinese government that is using its lust for profits against the United States, while America's political leadership looks on.

Even some of the most admired younger American technology corporations—the ones held up as examples of our continuing success and our unbeatable competitive edge—seem more and more loyal to China when you review the details. They turn out either not to create significant numbers of jobs or to create far more jobs in China than here. As media executive Leo Hindery Jr. blogged on the website of the Union of the Unemployed (UCubed), Facebook has only 2,000 employees. Twitter has 350. Cisco Systems and Oracle have roughly 180,000 combined—a substantial number, but half of those are now offshore. Apple, the brand beloved by consumers and praised by President Barack Obama as the future of American manufacturing, has only 25,000 employees in America and another 25,000 overseas. But what's rarely mentioned is that Apple's most admired products are not made here. A company called Foxconn Technology Group, with more than 1 million employees, makes them in China. A quarter million Foxconn workers do nothing but make Apple products. As Hindery explained, for every US employee of Apple working in marketing or product development, there are ten Foxconn workers in China making the iPads, iPhones, and iPods. And according to *Tax Notes*, a weekly publication from the nonprofit organization Tax Analysts, between 1999 and 2008, overall employment at the foreign affiliates of US parent companies increased an astounding 30 percent to 10.1 million, while US employment at American multinational corporations declined 8 percent to 21.1 million.

In other words, when we talk about "China" taking American jobs and doing the manufacturing that used to be done here, the truth is that we are talking about the choices of US-based multinational companies. The Chinese manipulations of tariffs and currency mean that the most profitable thing an American-based multinational can do is turn into a kind of trading pirate, flying the flag of the United States but making its money by plundering us instead. So America gets the bragging rights for Apple, but China gets ten times the Apple jobs.

Is Our Future in iPod City?

What does the new global manufacturing center look like? What is it like to work for Apple's biggest manufacturing partner, Foxconn? It turns out that it looks a lot like US manufacturing—but in the nineteenth century, before safety, labor, environmental, and consumer protection laws were in place, and when abuse of workers was common and industrial accidents like underground mine explosions were routine.

Two *New York Times* profiles of life in "iPod City" provided a glimpse. They described workers aged eighteen to twenty-four toiling twelve hours a day, six or seven days a week, for seventy-five cents an hour. Each employee endlessly repeated a specific task: for instance, a minute-long series of tests and adjustments to a hard drive moving down the assembly line. Although workers were permitted to speak to one another, they could not indulge in any "distractions," such as playing iPods. Foxconn management believes that such products lead workers to engage in "unproductive movements" that harm efficiency.

A report prepared by twenty Chinese universities described iPod City as a "labor camp" with extensive employee abuse, but that doesn't capture what it's like. Foxconn made international headlines in 2010 when young workers in the company dormitories started attempting suicide, some of them when Apple executives were touring the plant. In all, according to *Wired* magazine, seventeen workers died. The company responded by increasing wages to above $1 an hour, on average, and installing suicide-prevention nets to catch jumpers before they hit the ground. Suicide nets do not address the reasons that employees try to kill themselves; they only spare corporate executives at Foxconn and Apple the public embarrassment of explaining additional worker suicides inside their factories. Catching them when they jump—welcome to the new global manufacturing center.

We may shake our heads at stories of those unfortunate young iSlaves and perhaps feel a bit superior because in the United States, we don't treat our citizens this way. But before we congratulate ourselves, we'd better notice that not only do US-based multinational corporations profit from the conditions in those workplaces but also that they fail to make improvements. This is the "disinflation" that the president of the Dallas Fed bragged about. It's what he meant when he talked about his CEO friends who were frustrated because they could not "exploit globalization" fast enough.

The policy machinations happen on the other side of the Pacific, not just in America. In March 2006, write Brendan Smith, Tim Costello, and Jeremy Brecher in *Asia Times,* the Chinese government proposed a new labor law that would have improved working conditions moderately. In response, the American Chamber of Commerce in Shanghai, as well as US corporations such as General Electric, Wal-Mart, and even Google lobbied against the law, and in some cases threatened to leave China for countries such as Pakistan and Thailand if it passed. By December, the Chinese government had revised the draft law to limit workers' rights in the areas of contracts, collective bargaining, and severance, among others. The story's authors quote Scott Slipy, Microsoft's director of human resources in

China, who explained the change in the draft law in an interview with *BusinessWeek:* "We have enough investment at stake that we can usually get someone [in the Chinese government] to listen to us."

Foxconn USA?

When greedy bastards in a multinational corporation ship American jobs overseas, it's not just a benefit to the corporation and to the Chinese economy. As I mentioned before, it also strengthens the power of greedy bastards in America to lower US wages. The strategy is deliberate. As Smith, Brecher, and Costello observe, now that one in four industrial workers in the world is Chinese, "Chinese wages and conditions set those around the world not only in low-wage industries but increasingly in those with the highest of modern technology. Low wages and poor working conditions in China drive down those in the rest of the world in a 'race to the bottom.'"

You can see the sad finish line of this race in Danville, Virginia, where Swedish furniture maker Ikea opened a factory that sounds like it is run by Foxconn management. As Nathaniel Popper wrote in the *Los Angeles Times*, "Laborers in Swedwood plants [as IKEA's plants are known] in Sweden produce bookcases and tables similar to those manufactured in Danville. The big difference is that the Europeans enjoy a minimum wage of about $19 an hour and a government-mandated five weeks of paid vacation. Full-time employees in Danville start at $8 an hour with 12 vacation days—eight of them on dates determined by the company." A third of the Danville employees are paid as temporary workers, so their wages are even lower, and they receive no benefits at all.

Some US politicians are starting to argue that America can

Trade

The goal of the connect the dots in trade is to show how capital (money and human resources) is diverted away from one nation to another artificially using currency and tax policy.

Currency
China in 1994 sets its currency at 50 percent of US dollar.

50%

Where does the trade river flow?

Taxes
China taxes US imports at 25 percent. The US taxes China at only 2.5 percent.

Short-Term Results
• Big corporate profits
• Cheap US imports
• Massive US domestic job and investment extraction

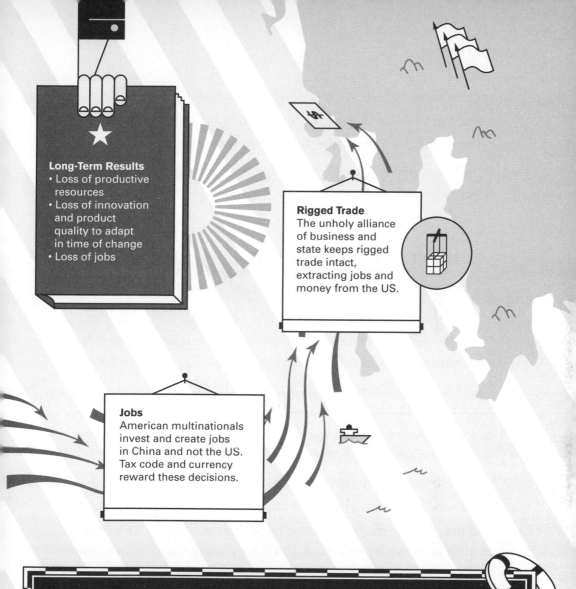

Long-Term Results
- Loss of productive resources
- Loss of innovation and product quality to adapt in time of change
- Loss of jobs

Rigged Trade
The unholy alliance of business and state keeps rigged trade intact, extracting jobs and money from the US.

Jobs
American multinationals invest and create jobs in China and not the US. Tax code and currency reward these decisions.

THE FIX

How to "Reset" the Game as they have before. Use the leverage of China's dependence on US marketplace and need for US debt repayment to negotiate change.

1 End rigged currency. President Reagan did this with the Plaza Accord in 1985 with Japan.

2 End unfair tax policy. President Nixon resolved unfair tax policy with Japan 1971.

3 Expose American CEOs who exploit the unholy alliance by lobbying to keep trade rigged.

4 Pass constitutional amendment getting money out of politics.

and should operate as a low-cost labor base with no environmental restrictions. Governor Rick Scott of Florida has talked about competing with China by gutting labor and environmental regulations. If China is becoming the new America of manufacturing, must America become the old China?

When "Free Trade" Isn't

Because of this unholy alliance between multinational business and the United States government, the "free market" for international trade is not an open competition, it's a rigged game, with the losers and winners determined in advance. On the losing end, we have the people and the long-term productivity of the United States. With shriveled investment from industry, private investors, and banks, America is left with slow growth, a shortage of new jobs, and fewer small business loans and home loans. Lower overall tax revenue means less money for infrastructure, education, and police and firemen, and fewer taxpayers to pay for the costs of government and ballooning deficits. As conservative pundit Stephen Moore explained in the *Wall Street Journal*, "If you want to understand better why so many states—from New York to Wisconsin to California— are teetering on the brink of bankruptcy, consider this depressing statistic: today in America there are nearly twice as many people working for the government (22.5 million) than in all of manufacturing (11.5 million). This scenario is an almost exact reversal of the situation in 1960, when there were 15 million workers in manufacturing and 8.7 million collecting a paycheck from the government." With so many good jobs moving abroad, government offers an ever larger percentage of the secure jobs that are left—until the government runs out of money, too. Wright contends that the number of government employees is the problem, but the real culprit is that our manufacturing jobs have gone overseas.

"American" multinationals plunder the capital from their home country to make money in China and elsewhere. This is the reason that CEOs can feel so confident, as I mentioned at the start of the book, while ordinary Americans see the country headed in the wrong direction. The CEOs are enriching themselves by driving the United States in the wrong direction. It serves their interests, but their interests are no longer aligned with the interests of most Americans, who are left with fewer jobs, especially high-quality jobs, and drive their kids to underfunded schools over pothole-strewn roads.

Financing Trade: Banks, Trade, and Politicians

Who else benefits? Let's go back to the FOMC for a second, that committee of policy makers that runs American monetary policy. Who exactly picked Dallas Federal Reserve president Richard Fisher to enact economic policy? Bankers. Yes, as we've seen, regional Federal Reserve banks, like the one in Dallas, are legally governed by a board of directors composed of regional banks. So Fisher is representing banks, and banks do very well in a world with enormous international capital flows.

On a very basic level, what bankers want is for the price of labor to go down. That's because they have money, and if you can buy more labor for the same amount of money, you are effectively richer and more powerful. So, they want to make sure that prices don't inflate too much. At the same time, they want wages to deflate. With lower prices and lower wages, workers get a smaller slice of American economic output, while corporations get to keep more and more. This is indeed what has happened, as workers' share of the economy's fruits is at record lows. So shipping off American jobs to China, while ensuring that workers back home have no bargaining power, is good for bankers.

On another level, banks make a lot of money mediating international capital flows. Big companies that want to invest in China, pension funds that want to move money around the world, hedge funds that want investment opportunity, and so on—all of this is highly profitable to banks. More trading agreements protecting the rights of investors also help banks find ways to funnel money through tax havens such as Singapore and Hong Kong that allow them to avoid paying US, local, and state taxes.

Banks have bought both political parties, and the politicians who receive contributions from those multinational trade vampires continue the favorable trade policies that help make them easy money. Politicians also get contributions from banksters who profit both on the Chinese deals and by investing their own money in China. It's more profitable for the trade vampires and the banksters to invest in China and pay off the American politicians than it is for them to invest in America. It pays short term. And like any other kind of criminal, bankers will keep committing the same crime as long as it pays.

Now, you might say that it's a good thing that American banks profit on their investments. Or at least bankers would. You might say that a banker's desire to get rich on overseas lending is reasonable. After all, shouldn't an independent businessperson, in a bank or anywhere else, be free to get rich as he or she chooses? Bankers talk about the need for international competitiveness, and normally I'd be somewhat sympathetic to this argument. Except that *the big banks aren't independent businesses.* Taxpayers like you and me subsidize the big banks in multiple ways. We pay for them with our tax money, some of which goes to the banks in the form of zero-interest loans. We pay for it with more of our tax money when the government guarantees that banks won't fail, even if they make bad loans. These government guarantees, backed by taxpayer money, raise the banks' credit ratings. They're a safer bet because we are available to bail them out. As a result, according to John Carney of CNBC.com, "the higher credit ratings make it cheaper for the banks to borrow—which means that the US taxpayer is essentially subsidizing them with an implicit guarantee. This is worth billions to the banks."

The reason that the banks get all this taxpayer money—and, in fact, the reason we have a Federal Reserve Bank system at all—is to promote growth: to benefit America's economy for Americans. Banks get taxpayer money and special privileges for the same reason that the police and the firefighters do: because they serve the public good. For a banker to use taxpayer money to send jobs and investment out of the United States is an outrageous betrayal of the entire system. It is pirating American capital for personal gain. If a business wants a corporate subsidy, then it has to accept the terms of the subsidy. Otherwise it's just taking money under false pretenses, which is also known as stealing.

It's as if the American taxpayer paid for a police force and armed it with guns, and then the police decided, "You know what? Now that we have these guns, we can make more money as robbers than as police. So hand over your wallets and your jewelry, but when you get home, please keep paying our salaries!"

And it's not just tax payments that bankroll greedy bastards destroying America. It's our own personal savings and our retirement accounts, a large portion of which are invested with the trading pirates we deplore. With little choice on our part, my mom and myself are investing in the destruction of America. How about your family?

The Threat from China

The biggest winner, though, is not our banks or our multinational corporations. What is utterly absurd about our current situation is that the biggest beneficiary of American trade and banking policies is not even American.

The biggest winner, short term, is the Chinese government. It enjoys sky-high economic growth, which has a whole list of benefits. First, increasing prosperity keeps Chinese workers under control, and pays for the police actions, Chinese media control, and narrowly targeted raises and subsidies the government metes out when discontented workers protest.

China is following a long-term strategy. It wants foreign investment, but more than that, it wants to make what the foreign companies make, with its own factories employing its own people. China is the leader among governments that use trade policy to move not just jobs but also entire industries from the United States to their own countries.

But there's a big risk here for Chinese leaders. In addition to manufacturing the goods that we buy, China is also the largest foreign holder of American debt. That means China depends on us twice over—to buy their goods, thereby creating their jobs, and to repay the money we've borrowed. Until now, our trade relationship has been a lose-lose proposition for the United States, but if we were to default on those debts, China would lose both its investments and biggest marketplace.

Ironically, the only way that China's greediest bastards will survive in the long run is if they demand that China end its own currency rigging and engage in direct collaboration with the United States to resolve tax and other trade issues. Because in the long run, America has the same interests as China. We all need to be long-term greedy. We all need to get back to playing Make a Cup.

How to Fight Back

Republicans and Democrats talk about standing up to China, but both sides get it wrong. Either because of the lobbyists' influence or because politicians don't understand China's larger strategy, US politicians tend to respond either by fighting in the name of "free trade" or by fighting to protect specific industries that are losing jobs and investment to Chinese competitors. But neither approach will stop China from realizing its long-term goals.

As Ian Fletcher wrote in The Huffington Post, our trade negotiators and diplomats were never trained to fight the long-term trade war that China is fighting. Instead, he says, they have "a hazy, almost undergraduate sense that 'economics says free trade is best.'" But China and like-minded countries are not interested in free trade. They are not practicing it, and nothing in international law can force them to do so. International trade law, Fletcher writes, is like "a game of stickball being played by children on a vacant lot: its rules only mean anything insofar as they are enforced by the players themselves."

When American negotiators fight in the name of greater trade "freedom," they just give the powerful players more freedom to rig the game in favor of their own countries and aligned businesses and banks. International trade is a game without a referee, and the only way to compete is to fight for our own interests just as hard as China fights for its interests. Or as Andrew Liveris of Dow Chemical has put it, America must "get in the game to win." But how can we do that when the interests of our politicians and our people are not aligned? Remember that the lawmakers' reelections depend on money from those businesses benefitting short term from the current setup.

When our politicians try to protect this or that industry suffering from unfair trade policies, their efforts are easily blocked. Economist Irwin Stelzer gives the example of President Obama's goal of doubling exports in five years. Sounds like a good idea, doesn't it? Westinghouse helped reach that goal when it won a contract to sell nuclear stations to China. GE did the same with a deal to manufacture turbine plants for wind power. However, Stelzer reports, the Chinese insisted "that this and other deals include a turnover of all technology." Using the new American technology, Chinese companies began copying our products and supplying them to state-owned companies, which are required by law to buy from Chinese companies. In this way, American technology seeds new Chinese industries that can then compete, with unfair advantages, against American industry. In the end, we get a short-term increase in exports, while China gets entirely new industries based on technologies it took us decades to develop.

How to Stop the Trade Pirates

Free trade isn't the answer. Protectionism isn't the answer. So how do we end rigged trade? "If we continue to let markets rule in every instance," Andrew Liveris explains in his book, *Make It in America*, "we will become the global economy's biggest bystander, and potentially its biggest drain. . . . It is time for us to recognize, whether we like it or not, that for now, in certain key areas, we actually need more government, not less." What would a pro-America, activist government—and its citizens—do to end rigged trading?

FIGHT BACK ON CURRENCY MANIPULATION. We must insist on transparency about what China does. The country spends 10 percent of its gross domestic product (GDP) buying dollars to keep the yuan low. Our government could formally declare China a currency manipulator and be ready to impose sanctions if its government doesn't respond. According to Jared Bernstein, former chief economist to Vice President Joe Biden, immediate action must be taken, either by Congress or directly by the president. In 2010 the House of Representatives passed legislation to strengthen the government's hand, but despite bipartisan support for the bill in the House, the Senate failed to act due to the influence of multinational corporations. If we care about the future productivity of this country, we need to hold our representatives responsible for it. As Thea Lee, deputy chief of staff at the AFL-CIO (American Federation of Labor and Congress of Industrial Organizations), put it, when it comes to Chinese currency manipulation, "We need our own government to do its job."

In 1985, Ronald Reagan ended forty years of Japanese mercantilism in currency manipulation. In one weekend at New York's Plaza Hotel, the president won an agreement with the governments of France, West Germany, Japan, and the United Kingdom that lowered the value of the dollar against the yen by more than 50 percent in two years. The president did not reach all of his goals with this approach, but it can be combined with other political tools.

FIGHT BACK ON TARIFFS. As with currency policy, China's tax policy is a weapon in an ongoing trade war. Until the United States meets this force with an equal force, we will not be able to reestablish America as a place where industry would choose to invest over China. In 1971 President Richard Nixon imposed across-the-board surcharges on Japanese imports, and four months after this show of force, he negotiated a new exchange rate with Japan.

Why not do the same with China today?

REVEAL THE REAL PRICE OF RIGGED TRADE. Chinese companies have been allowed to shift costs to the US government and the American people in a variety of ways that are difficult to see. First, the United States sets standards for safety, quality, and environmental protection that Chinese companies routinely ignore. Rob Dumont, president of the Tooling, Manufacturing & Technologies Association, a national trade association representing small manufacturers, gave the example of an Alabama steel manufacturer losing orders to a cheaper Chinese competitor. As Dumont told a forum sponsored by the Coalition for a Prosperous America, the US manufacturer "sent a fact-finding team to China and discovered that not only did the plant have no environmental controls, but the lab that was supposed to certify the steel grade didn't even have the equipment to properly conduct the tests." Meanwhile, a lab in the United States confirmed that the steel shipped from China did not meet its specifications for quality and strength.

Think about how many ways that purchasing inferior steel could cost Americans. There were the orders lost by the company, the jobs lost by its workers as the company struggled against unfair competition, the expense to taxpayers for having regulators test the quality of Chinese goods, and the costs that could come from inferior steel failing after it was installed in a building—or even in a nuclear power plant. As Peter Navarro and Greg Autry write in *Death by China: Confronting the Dragon—A Global Call to Action*, consumers as well as corporations should recognize that the low price tags on Chinese goods don't necessarily signify a bargain but a distraction from the price we pay in other ways. "Cheap," they point out, "isn't always the cheapest."

There is one more hidden cost, a cost that all of us are paying. That is the cost of blaming China instead of working to rebuild America. Politicians giving speeches and appearing on television find that China bashing makes for a popular talking point. It vents frustration and makes us feel that the politicians are on our side, fighting the evil foreign enemy. The truth is that China is only doing what US politicians and US CEOs of American-based multinational corporations allow and profiting from it.

The greedy-bastard politicians and private executives offer something that, on the surface, seems appealing. As we ship manufacturing jobs off to China, budget-crunched Americans get to enjoy the benefit of lifestyle upgrades by buying cheap Chinese products.

American consumers save money, but with a dangerous long-term cost that doesn't show up at the cash register.

The United States loses old jobs but does not invest in creating new ones as money gets invested elsewhere. America borrows trillions to support banks that make it easy for consumers to keep buying cheap imported goods. As the United States borrows, it "prints" money and slowly drops the value of the dollar worldwide—in the process driving up the worldwide cost (in dollars) of everything from oil and wheat to corn and copper.

For a while, the greedy bastards in the Chinese government and corporations get rich and keep power. Meanwhile, employment rises in China as it falls in the United States. Unlike the newfangled extractions seen in banking, trade extraction has been practiced for centuries. A simple misalignment of interests among state government, wealth, and the people enriches a few while harming the long-term prosperity of us all.

Health Care Without Health

When I was growing up, I used to hear adults say, "You get what you pay for." They meant that if you spend good money on anything from a pair of shoes to a house, you will get good quality in return—and if you spend less, you'll receive less. By that measure, United States citizens should be, by far, the healthiest and longest lived in the history of the world. We spend more than twice as much on medical care than the next most prosperous countries. We spend

so much, in fact, and the costs are so damaging to us that it can be hard to believe. How much? As of now, America spends roughly 16 percent of its national wealth on health care annually. Each year, for every $6 in an American's wallet or bank account, $1 will go to pay for health care.

What do we get for our money? According to the CIA, we rank fiftieth in life expectancy, behind countries such as Greece, Portugal, and Bosnia and Herzegovina. Our health care outcomes are comparable to countries such as Chile. But to keep up with Chile, according to the research from the French bank Société Générale, we spend more than *seven times as much as it does*—more than $7,000 per person per year, as compared with less than $1,000 in Chile. An astonishing 20 to 30 percent of our money goes to bureaucracy and paperwork. Countries such as Singapore and the Czech Republic spend less on all of medical care than we spend on administrative costs, yet those two countries rate just about where we do on measures of life expectancy and "healthy life" expectancy, which considers quality of life and not just length.

Our health insurance costs have risen twice as fast as inflation since 1980. The waste and theft in the health care industry are now so enormous, and health-related costs eat up so much of government budgets at every level, they are depriving us of funds to pay for other community essentials such as teachers and police. Dr. David Ludwig, author of *Ending the Food Fight*, has observed that "the $4 trillion that the Republicans want to cut [from the federal budget] over a decade is about the same as the projected costs of diabetes over that same period." That's simply outrageous. The rising costs associated with just one largely preventable disease threaten to cost us more than we would save under the most severe federal cost-cutting plan ever proposed.

When you spend far too much on any one thing, you limit what you can spend for anything else. The state of Massachusetts voted to allocate an extra $1 billion to its public school system to reduce class size and increase teacher pay, but as Atul Gawande, a surgeon and staff writer at *The New Yorker* writes, "Every dollar ended up being diverted to covering rising health care costs. For each dollar added to school budgets, the costs of maintaining teacher health benefits took a dollar and forty cents." And this was no isolated incident. Gawande observes that this is "a story found in every state." When journalist Joe Wiesenthal of the website Business Insider reported on the SocGen study cited above, he titled his article, "Forget Medicare, *This* Is the Chart That Shows Why America Is Doomed."

I don't accept that we're doomed, but I have come to see health care as a greedy-bastard paradise of misaligned interests, an example of an industry rigged to suck capital out of our pockets for private gain. The incentives for everyone involved—from doctors, hospitals, drug companies, and insurance companies, to the employers who provide the majority of health insurance coverage and even the unions that represent workers—are not just out of alignment, they're backward. They reward waste and punish efficiency. To see this corrupt system at work, simply follow a patient through the system.

First, You See a Doctor

The point of seeing a doctor—or being one—ought to be improved health. After all, besides your mom or spouse, who do you count on to care about your well-being more than your doctor does?

And while many good people become physicians and feel a powerful moral calling to serve their patients, the traditional fee-for-service model of payment fights against that moral calling with every exam a doctor performs.

I'll use a friend of mine as an example. Call him Larry. His work required him to spend increasing amounts of time at the computer, both in his office and on the road. He began to have tingling pain in his right wrist. Sometimes he felt it up his arm, even when he wasn't typing. At a regular checkup with his primary care doctor, he asked about the pain, which came and went. "I'm not a hand specialist," his doctor said, "but it looks like a repetitive strain injury." Larry told his doctor about all the computer work he'd been doing, and his doctor gave him some practical lifestyle suggestions. To cut down on time at the keyboard, he could use dictation software. When typing was necessary, he could make sure that his workstation and his posture matched health guidelines. The doctor mentioned in passing that one common yoga position had been shown in studies to help as well.

The conversation lasted only a couple of minutes, and Larry left with good intentions. But he had never thought of himself as a yoga person, and he never made it to a class. Changing your lifestyle actually takes a fair amount of work, mental preparation, and coaching, none of which he got from our medical system. Soon he was back to his old habits at the keyboard—long hours, few breaks, bad posture—and the conversation with his doctor faded from his mind. Then the shooting pain and the swelling in his wrist began to wake him in the middle of the night. Some days he couldn't type at all. His work suffered. Now his injury seemed like an emergency, and he scheduled a meeting with a hand specialist. She took X-rays and confirmed a repetitive stress injury called a ganglion cyst. She told

Larry that she could operate on the cyst, a small sac of fluid located under the skin. Larry was uncertain; was surgery really necessary? Hadn't he been told that he might solve the problem with rest, better posture, and a more ergonomic workstation?

The hand specialist told him that as far as she was concerned, the treatment for his condition was surgery but that the decision was his. A few days later, her office called to let him know that she had a cancelation in her schedule. He could come into her office for the outpatient procedure that week. Larry agreed. He felt fortunate because his medical insurance covered the cost of the surgery.

There are two points to this story. The first is that both doctors were right. Both courses of treatment prove successful for many patients, though neither guaranteed success. But the second point is that all the incentives for doctors cut against low-cost preventive care and in favor of expensive tests and surgery. The first doctor spent only a little time talking to Larry about the lifestyle changes he might have made, but that's not surprising. We pay doctors little for talking with patients. Instead, they earn the biggest fees when they perform the most demanding and high-tech services: tests and procedures. The bread and butter of fee-for-service doctors is a patient who is sick or suffering acutely, and they make the most money when they can do what Larry's hand specialist did: conduct tests and procedures in their own offices, where they own the equipment and keep all of the profits.

Fee-for-service is not really a health care system, it's a *treatment sales system*: the more tests and treatments a doctor can sell, the more fees he or she can collect. This system creates a constant pressure for hospitals and doctors to order unnecessary procedures, putting health care professionals at odds with their own patients and driving up costs. What we get are more frequent and more expensive medical interventions, but what we want is to be healthier so that we need *fewer* medical interventions. During the months of heated debate about President Obama's health care plan, former Democratic National Committee chairman (and onetime family practitioner) Dr. Howard Dean told me, "Fee-for-service payment systems may be the single biggest barrier to controlling health care costs in America."

Since many of the tests and procedures are unnecessary, but the patient often doesn't see the bill, this creates an enormous incentive for fraud. The National Health Care Anti-Fraud Association, a Washington, DC-based group of health insurers and state and federal law enforcement officials, estimates that at least 3 percent of all health care spending—or $68 billion a year—is lost to fraud. In South Florida, CBS News reported that the Medicare fraud business is now bigger than the illegal drug trade.

In Larry's case, both possible courses of treatment were medically reasonable. However, there was a subtle pressure on the doctors, a creeping greedy bastardism so familiar to American patients that they may not even notice it. Larry might have benefitted from more time to talk with his doctor, and more specific instructions about the changes he could make at home and at work to relieve the strain on his wrist. He might have benefitted from follow-up phone calls and other encouragement to stick with such changes. In fact, he might have solved his problem without going under the knife, taking sick days away from his job, and running up a substantial bill. But who in this country imagines that a doctor would follow up to see if Larry was working on his posture while typing, or going to his beginner yoga class—even if that could prevent a surgery? The surgery is what pays.

Next, You Get a Bill

Before Larry underwent surgery, he was charged a copayment. Afterward, he didn't even see a bill, and he didn't worry about the details. Insurance "covered" it. Who created that bill? The process probably went this way: His doctor dictated the details of the care that Larry had received. Then a paid transcriber typed up her notes. Then a paid coder translated the typed description into medical shorthand codes. Then a paid medical biller wrote up the codes as a bill that was sent to the insurance company. Then an insurance adjuster reviewed the bill and authorized full or partial payment.

You can see in this progression of paid bureaucrats how it is that 20 percent to 30 percent of our health care dollars go to the paperwork bureaucracy. The data are clear. In 1999 the United States spent $1,059 per person on health care administration, versus $307 per person in Canada. Of that, $259 went to insurance companies (mostly to private insurance; Medicare and Medicaid have very low overhead), $315 to hospitals, and $324 to doctors. Today those numbers are much higher. Keep in mind that this is not spending on health care, it is spending on shuffling paper around.

And you can see something else as well: even when honest doctors generate bills for necessary services, the process requires a long game of telephone among people all paid to work as quickly as possible. Let's assume that these professionals are all well trained and committed to doing a good job. With whom are their interests aligned? "The transcriptionist, the coder, and the biller will take great care to avoid erring against their physician employer," wrote independent medical billing advocate Dennis Grace. "Any error that hurts the doctor potentially damages their livelihood. But aren't they concerned about the patients? Aren't patients the real source of everyone's income? Sure, but most patients will never see a detailed bill, never look at the surgeon's operating notes, never decode their bills."

Like medicine itself, medical billing is a complicated system with lots of opportunity for error, performed by people who get paid when the doctor sells exams, tests, and procedures—not when the patient gets healthy. There is no penalty for overcharging a patient. So it should not come as a surprise that Medical Billing Advocates of America, a national association that checks medical bills for consumers, says eight out of ten hospital bills its members scrutinize contain errors. Bills from doctors' offices and labs tend to have fewer mistakes, but errors are common there, too.

Who Sets These Prices?

I'm not trying to pick on doctors. But remember the premise of Trade a Cup, where bad actors drive out the good. In many cases, physicians simply have no choice but to work within the system. Even an honest doctor paid by fee-for-service within an honest and accurate billing bureaucracy will still unwittingly overcharge his or her patients. For over a century, the American Medical Association has influenced Congress to maintain an artificial shortage of doctors. As Dennis Cauchon reported in *USA Today*, "The marketplace doesn't determine how many doctors the nation has, as it does for engineers, pilots, and other professions. The number of doctors is a political decision, heavily influenced by doctors themselves." Back in 1910 the AMA commissioned the *Flexner Report*, which claimed that many medical schools produced poor-quality doctors. Based on the report, the AMA convinced Congress to shut down many medical schools, reducing the number of doctors by 30 percent over thirty years. More recently, since the 1980s, few new medical schools have been allowed to open, and Congress, which requires that all physicians (even experienced doctors trained in other countries) complete medical residencies, has set a cap of one hundred thousand residencies per year—a quota for new doctors. For decades, the AMA warned about the threat of a "doctor glut," and only the recent, damaging shortage of physicians, especially for rural areas, compelled it to stop.

The AMA stifles competition even further by using its political influence to prevent nondoctors such as nurses, physician's assistants, and alternative medicine practitioners from providing services such as midwifery, acupuncture, and massage therapy that might compete with holders of a medical school degree. This system is a classic greedy-bastard manipulation of government to alter market structure and reduce choice to keep prices high. This tactic worked well for John D. Rockefeller with Standard Oil, and it works well for the AMA and countless other greedy bastards.

Shikha Dalmia, a senior policy analyst for the nonprofit think tank Reason Foundation, described in *Forbes* how the AMA used its political influence to insist that only doctors could deliver babies, even though midwives have performed this service for years. "Midwifery, once a robust industry in this country, has been virtually destroyed, thanks to the intense lobbying against it by the medical industry. In 1995 thirty-six states restricted or outright banned midwifery, even though studies have found that it delivers equally safe care at far lower prices than standard hospital births." This is still going on: the midwife-run Bellevue Hospital Birthing Center in New York City, which had one of the city's lowest rates of Cesarean sections despite its caseload of Medicaid-assisted poor mothers, was shut down in 2010. The birthing center emphasized inexpensive natural birthing techniques rather than high-tech monitoring and surgery. It wasn't shut down because it didn't work, so say advocates, but because it worked too well. Each time the AMA and the system that privileges expensive inefficient care over lower-cost but equally effective care enforces this monopolistic system, consumers pay more—and lose another health care choice.

A further cause of unnecessarily high prices for medical procedures is malpractice lawsuits—though not mainly for the reason you may have heard about in the bogus debates of our political theater. Some critics of unnecessary lawsuits make it sound as if eliminating large awards for medical malpractice would bring down the cost of health care, but as a percentage of our overall medical costs, lawsuits are small. Doing away with them would deprive the system of an important force for visibility (lawsuits reveal what the worst medical providers are doing) and aligned interests (lawsuits pressure medical providers to take better care of their patients). But when you combine our current legal arrangements with the fee-for-service system, a serious problem results. The threat of being sued puts pressure on medical providers to run more tests and perform more procedures, so they can't be sued for failing to provide a necessary service. This creates a second reason for doctors to provide services we don't need: in addition to greed, there is also the motivation of fear. To my eye, that's not a reason to forbid lawsuits, but to end the fee-for-service model that rewards both bad motivations for unnecessary spending.

What If You Need a Prescription?

Larry went home after his surgery with prescriptions for a painkiller and an antibiotic to prevent infection. In doing so, he contributed to the $4 trillion that Americans will spend on prescription drugs over the next ten years, or roughly $10,000 for every person in the country, according to research from the Centers for Medicare and Medicaid Services. But this level of spending on drugs happens only here. In much of the rest of the world, prescription drugs are simply not that expensive. Why the enormous difference? There are three reasons. First, drugs are purchased mainly by the private insurance companies and the government (through Medicare). In other words, drugs are frequently sold with one buyer and no competition, like planes to the Defense Department. This lack of open competition keeps prices high.

Second, drug prices are protected by patent laws. The founders of this country recognized that innovation can be slow to pay off. They wanted to guarantee that scientists and inventors had the financial incentives to pursue long-term creative work. For that reason, Article 1, Section 8 of the US Constitution, which was conceived by Thomas Jefferson, gives Congress the power "to promote the progress of science and useful arts, by securing for limited times to authors and inventors the exclusive right to their respective writings and discoveries." This protection is otherwise known as a patent.

America has invested in drug development, publicly and privately, more than any other nation in the world. According to the Organization for Economic Cooperation and Development (OECD), direct US government support for health-related research and development represented 0.22 percent of our GDP in 2008. That sounds small, but it translates into almost three-quarters of all government-funded health-related R&D among *all* the thirty-four member countries of the OECD. That's our money. Other countries benefit from our decades of research and billions spent in capital from academic institutions and the National Institutes of Health. Increased costs for pharmaceuticals in the United States compared with other countries means that Americans pay for the cost of the research subsidies and tax credits for drug companies, footing the bill for the innovation that leads to an eventual product. Others, meanwhile, get to pay just for the product. Over time, this sensible attempt to support American innovation has been captured by the unholy alliance between business and state, which has created a third cause of price inflation. There are now not one but three different ways that the government grants protections to drug companies against competition. The first is known as a patent, which goes through the US Patent and Trademark Office. The second is "market exclusivity," in which the US Food and Drug Administration agrees not to accept any applications for competing drugs for a period of time. And the third is "data exclusivity," in which the company can own the safety and efficacy data required for FDA approval; if another manufacturer wants to develop a competing drug, it must generate its own safety data, an expensive proposition.

The politics here get messy. Washington is an endless battlefield of regulations and patents that control who can sell which drugs. But overall, the political battles have paid off for the drug makers. In 2004, according to *Time* magazine, "the pharmaceutical industry topped the list of the most profitable industries, with a return of 17% on revenue." In 2010 the pharmaceutical industry had worldwide sales of $860 billion.

How much difference does it make for the patient? And how

do some drug companies turn critical rights like patent protection for drug developers into easy extraction—staving off competition from lower-priced generics, for example—without inventing anything new?

Let's look at a hormonal agent called hydroxyprogesterone. For decades, it has been used by obstetricians to treat pregnant women at risk of premature birth, but this was an "off-label" use not approved by the FDA or reimbursed by insurance. In February 2011, the FDA granted approval to a company called KV Pharmaceutical to sell the hormone as a regulated drug under the brand name Makena. Now, KV Pharmaceutical had the exclusive right to sell this hormonal agent. They hiked the price from $15 per injection to $1,500 per injection. Since fifteen to twenty injections are necessary per pregnancy, this increased the price from roughly $300 to $25,000, all going straight to the bottom line of KV Pharmaceutical. There was no value added for anyone; it was pure extraction of capital from patients and taxpayers.

And as you probably expect by now, the drug companies' alliance with government not only jacks up prices but also wrecks the alignment of the incentives for everyone involved. Drug companies receive their biggest rewards for getting new compounds classified as "regulated drugs" and then marketing them ferociously until their monopoly runs out. When the day comes that other companies are allowed to make a competitive version of drug—so-called generic drugs—revenue will drop by roughly 90 percent. That's why we all constantly see those "Ask your doctor" advertisements hawking the newest medication. Drug companies do not get their biggest rewards by selling effective, quality medication but by selling politically protected medicine as fast as possible before the special legal protection expires. A constitutional protection that was supposed to align the interests of innovators with the nation as a whole too often now is perverted to use government protections as a cover for extraction.

Numbing the Financial Pain

Most Americans don't pay directly for most drugs they buy. In 1999, 69 percent of drugs were purchased by third-party buyers. There is a huge short-term incentive to hide the real cost of health care from voters to preserve power and make profits. Medicare Part D, which went into effect in 2006, for example, proposed and implemented by then president George W. Bush and a Republican-led Congress, created billions in unfunded payments to pharmaceutical companies for drugs for seniors. The companies' profits rose, and the AARP, the lobbying organization for senior citizens, endorsed it. It was a direct payoff, an attempt to lavish cash on both pharmaceutical companies as well as reward a major electoral constituent group: seniors. Fifty-four percent of voters age sixty and over, in turn, voted for Bush in 2004. The key here, once again, is that the system has distorted incentives.

Are you taking more drugs than you need? Pharmaceuticals provide useful treatments, but patients sometimes get prescribed medicine they don't need. Here too we see the logic of ongoing misallocation and corruption. In 2008, a study by Canadian researchers found that "With about 700,000 practicing physicians in the US in 2004, we estimate that with a total expenditure of US\$57.5 billion, the industry spent around US\$61,000 in promotion per physician." Drug companies underwrite more than half of doctors' continuing medical education. They use repeated visits by pharmaceutical sales reps (often bearing free lunches for the office staff) and freebie gifts to encourage physicians to prescribe their drugs. Doctors say that these small gifts and dinners have no effect, but behavioral research shows that even small favors create a reciprocal arrangement.

It doesn't stop there. In 2009, the *New York Times* reported that some drug companies were caught hiring ghostwriters to produce papers for top medical journals promoting their drugs under the names of prestigious doctors. Pharmaceuticals do tend to treat symptoms and diseases, but it's clear that if there's an incentive to overprescribe, people will get medicine they don't need for conditions they don't have. It is not healthy, but for the greedy bastards it is profitable.

The Cost of Insurance

Larry considered himself lucky because his insurance would "cover" his surgery. What he didn't consider was that he had already been overcharged enormously through expensive monthly premiums to the insurance company that paid for the operation. He had few real choices in buying health insurance, because it is a legally protected near monopoly. In some states, this monopoly is obvious. For example, in Maine, a company called Wellpoint controls 71 percent of the market. In Arkansas and Alabama, Blue Cross Blue Shield controls over 75 percent of the market. In 95 percent of the country, a single health care company controls at least 30 percent of the insurance market. But the industry's power to set prices is greater than those figures suggest, because it enjoys an exemption from the antitrust laws that stop other industries from fixing prices. The only business with this same exemption is Major League Baseball.

Senator Chuck Schumer of New York has called the health insurance industry's exemption, known as the McCarran-Ferguson Act of 1945, "one of the worst accidents of American history. It deserves the blame for the huge rise in premiums that has made health insurance so unaffordable." Hostility to the exemption crosses party lines. In 2007, Republican senator Trent Lott of Mississippi and Democratic senator Patrick Leahy of Vermont cosponsored legislation to repeal antitrust exemptions benefitting the insurance industry. "I cannot for the life of me understand why we have allowed this exemption to stay in place so long," Lott testified before the Senate Judiciary Committee.

But the exemption remains, leaving insurance companies free to fix prices. How do they maintain this privilege? With a lobbying effort greater than any industry except banking. In the first six months of 2009, for example, while the Obama health care reform was negotiated, health care companies spent $263 million on direct lobbying, according to Bloomberg news. Pharmaceutical companies alone spent $134 million. But even if you could wave a magic wand, end the antitrust exemption, and take all the lobbyists and other greedy bastards out of health care, private health insurance will always cost too much, spend too much on bureaucracy, and leave many citizens with no coverage at all. As British economist Tim Harford explained in *The Undercover Economist*, the free market can never give us what most of us would consider the right result: quality care for everyone who wants it at a fair price.

The problem is that health insurance is something we know we may not need for a long time. Lifetime spending is predictable: you need a little when you're young (immunizations, childhood illnesses, injuries), then you probably don't need a doctor much until you reach middle age, and possibly later (the exception being, of course, when women have children). The later stage of our lives is when the big expenses come. In a free market, where people are free to buy health insurance or not, some will bet that they don't need insurance or deny that they will ever become older and more frail. Because those people aren't paying into the system, the ones who remain have to pay more to cover the claims, driving the cost of insurance higher. As the price goes up further, it becomes an increasingly bad deal, and more people opt out either because they don't like the deal they're offered or because they're poor and can't afford high premiums even if they wish to pay. Indeed, as we'll see, the best and cheapest health care system is one that doesn't operate according to private market or government principles but simply aligns health professionals and people to seek health every day for their whole lives.

Of course, people who are already sick or elderly are most likely to stay in the system because they need it. Insurance companies will try to figure out who those people are, but that's expensive and time consuming—so in a free market, insurers trying to obtain accurate information about their customers will swell into big bureaucracies, and the price will go up even higher to cover that bureaucracy.

Think of car insurance. What if you could be reasonably sure that you could predict the years in which you would have accidents? Wouldn't you avoid paying for insurance until that year? That's the problem with health insurance: many people bet that they won't develop an illness or suffer a mishap this year, and the ones who are left in the system have to pay too much to keep it going.

We are the only country with a voluntary, primarily employer-sponsored health insurance system, and it will always be expensive (we spend more than any other country), bureaucratic (we spend more on paperwork and the people who process it than many countries spend on actual health care), and patchy (before the new health care law passed, 15 percent of Americans had no health care coverage, compared with just 0.2 percent in Germany). It will also create barriers to the best possible care, because decisions about what care you get must be negotiated with your insurer. In other words, if you come down with illness x and they cover drugs as treatment for x but not surgery, you'll be under financial pressure to take the drugs. If they change policy and pay for the surgery but not the drugs, you'll be under pressure to switch. Your care will always be some compromise between what you and your doctor think is best, and what insurance will cover.

Why Does Your Boss Have a Say in Your Health Care?

A further problem with employer-based health insurance is that when your employer picks your health insurance options for you, it is likely to serve its own interests as an employer, not yours as a patient. When it comes to your health, you and your employer simply don't have aligned interests. Making matters worse, employer-based health care constricts the economy by keeping people from leaving low-paying jobs or risking to work for new or small companies that don't offer health insurance. As with the housing slump, which prevents people from moving to areas of the country with better opportunities because they can't sell their homes, employer-based health insurance ties millions of American to poor jobs when the economy needs them to move and adapt, two key ingredients for economic growth and innovation.

In March 2011, I felt again just how scared Americans can feel about losing their employer-based health care, when the National Football League was negotiating with its players over revenue. The NFL had an arrangement where the league and the owners took

Health Care

Choices made to align the interests of health professionals and patients enhance health. Misaligned interests between health professionals and patients escalate health care costs and do little to promote health.

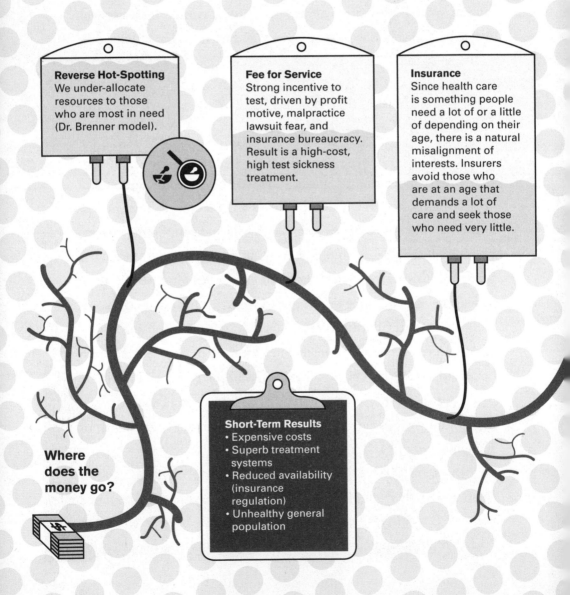

Reverse Hot-Spotting
We under-allocate resources to those who are most in need (Dr. Brenner model).

Fee for Service
Strong incentive to test, driven by profit motive, malpractice lawsuit fear, and insurance bureaucracy. Result is a high-cost, high test sickness treatment.

Insurance
Since health care is something people need a lot of or a little of depending on their age, there is a natural misalignment of interests. Insurers avoid those who are at an age that demands a lot of care and seek those who need very little.

Where does the money go?

Short-Term Results
• Expensive costs
• Superb treatment systems
• Reduced availability (insurance regulation)
• Unhealthy general population

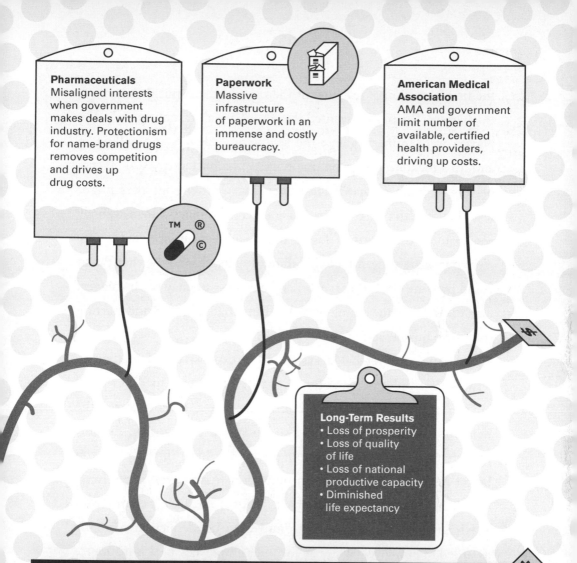

Pharmaceuticals
Misaligned interests when government makes deals with drug industry. Protectionism for name-brand drugs removes competition and drives up drug costs.

Paperwork
Massive infrastructure of paperwork in an immense and costly bureaucracy.

American Medical Association
AMA and government limit number of available, certified health providers, driving up costs.

Long-Term Results
- Loss of prosperity
- Loss of quality of life
- Loss of national productive capacity
- Diminished life expectancy

THE FIX

How to "Reset" the System as they have in places like Singapore. We can do better. Align incentives to create health.

1 Use hot-spotting by focusing preventative resources on the health care systems' "super-users." Identify those most in need earlier.

2 Replace fee-for-service with Mayo Clinic "group-based" salary model to align doctors and patients.

3 Mandate national Forced Savings Accounts for catastrophic health treatments where patients pay health professionals directly.

4 Subject drug companies to fair global competition.

5 Cloud computing.

6 End the unholy alliance.

the first $1 billion of revenue for themselves, then split the rest with the players. The players wanted them to share all revenue evenly. The players were unified against the league and owners and willing to endure a lockout, except on one point. As reported by AOL News, players were afraid that if the owners locked them out, they might lose their health care coverage. Of course, NFL players are extremely well paid. If the threat of losing their health insurance could scare *them* out of fighting for a half billion dollars, think how that threat could pressure the ordinary worker. That pressure may be the biggest barrier we have preventing workers from changing jobs and starting their own businesses.

If an employer-based system is so expensive and inefficient, why don't employers or unions fight it? Small and medium-sized businesses would like to get rid of the expense and benefit from the flexibility, but large employers like having an extra reason for employees to stick around. And unions, which have in the past won better health care benefits than nonunion workers can get, rely on health benefits to keep workers in unions. In 2009, Senator Ron Wyden of Oregon attempted to move the tax deduction currently awarded to employers who pay for their employees' health insurance to the workers themselves. Under Wyden's plan, citizens could use the government subsidy to purchase health care on a national exchange. But the idea was shot down during the legislative process.

It was Senator Max Baucus of Montana, a fellow Democrat, who helped shoot down Wyden. Of note, Baucus's chief adviser in this negotiation was a former private health insurance executive from Wellpoint. But it wasn't just insurance companies that opposed the change. Oregon unions attacked Wyden's idea with the inspiring phrase "We must protect the employer-based health care system that is already in existence." The status quo is powerful because it benefits greedy bastards.

Can Patients and Health Professionals Work Together?

Even with the interests of patients, insurers, and doctors terribly misaligned, there are still innovative Americans working on these questions and making impressive progress. These are people who recognize, as Mark Bittman put it, that what we have now is not a "health care" system, it's a "disease care" system. We reward the people who find the most ways to spend money on diseases and people's fears about them. What we want is a *health improvement system*, in which the rewards go to making people healthier and helping them stay that way. What might health care look like, and how would it work, if we got the incentives aligned to put the patient first? We're now going to look at some examples of where the incentives are aligned properly, and at one major system of public health care in the United States that serves millions of people with high-quality yet inexpensive care.

Let's start with what has actually been proven to cut costs and promote health at the same time. They call it "hot-spotting." Do you remember when former New York City police commissioner William Bratton revolutionized urban policing by mapping where and when crimes took place, and then sending extra police officers to the hot spots where the largest numbers of crimes were committed? By investing resources targeted at reducing crime in the worst areas at the worst times, Bratton found it was possible to lower crime overall. As Atul Gawande reported in *The New Yorker*, a New Jersey family doctor named Jeffrey Brenner studied data on where ambulances picked up patients in the city of Camden, New Jersey. He realized that what was true of crime was also true of medical costs: a large percentage of the problems came from a remarkably small number of places and people. In the case of Camden, just 1 percent of the patients—about a thousand people—incurred 30 percent of the health care costs.

It was not just that some patients are expensive. Brenner also found that "the people with highest medical costs—the people cycling in and out of the hospital—were usually the people receiving the worst care." Extra spending didn't deliver extra benefit. You didn't "get what you pay for." It was the opposite: high spending was often a sign of the system failing the patient. Brenner came to a surprising conclusion: "Emergency room visits and hospital admissions should be considered failures of the health care system until proven otherwise."

At first, that sounds crazy. How is admitting a patient into a hospital a failure of the system? Shouldn't it be the other way around: that the failure is when a patient in need can't get a hospital bed? Brenner's point is that a large number of people who wind up receiving expensive medical care could have gotten less drastic treatment but earlier and more often—as in the case of my friend Larry. Preventive care might have kept him from becoming injured severely enough to require surgery.

We have a *health care* industry that cares for the sick and injured by selling them treatments, but what would improve health most would be a separate *health* industry. As described to me by Dr. Jeff Spees, professor of medicine at the University of Vermont, in a private interview, our focus needs to expand beyond healing the sick. We need to provide education, coaching, and ongoing follow-up support in areas such as nutrition, exercise, and related personal practices. As Dr. Spees told me, "Some of the money that now goes to fee-for-service medicine could be directed to these preventive measures that preserve *health*, which would drive down the costs of *health care*." Keeping healthy people healthy would keep them out of the hands of the industry's greedy bastards.

Health Care the Right Way

Of course, some people will always become sick or injured, and health care will always have costs. But the high cost of health care may not be a tragic necessity. Instead, it may be a sign that for many patients we are providing care the wrong way. "For a thirty-year-old with a fever," Gawande explains, "a twenty-minute visit to the doctor's office may be just the thing. For a pedestrian hit by a mini-van, there's nowhere better than an emergency room. But these institutions are vastly inadequate for people with complex problems." Doctor visits and ERs were not designed to help people at risk for largely preventable conditions like our budget-busting diabetes epidemic. ERs were not designed to help people manage multiple illnesses with complex schedules of treatment and medication, as many elderly must do. For these reasons, two groups incur a high percentage of avoidable medical expenses: the poor, who can't afford preventive care, and the elderly, who can't get the help they need to manage their illnesses outside of a hospital. "The critical flaw in our health care system," Gawande concludes, "is that it was never designed for the kind of patients who incur the highest costs."

What sort of system would serve them better? Something like the Special Care Center in Atlantic City, New Jersey, a clinic designed for workers with extremely high medical expenses. Doctors are paid a flat monthly fee for each patient who belongs to the clinic, which not only gives them a financial incentive to keep people healthy, it also cuts out billing paperwork entirely, a substantial savings. Everything the clinic does is designed "around the things that sick, expensive patients most need and value," Gawande writes, "rather than the ones that pay the best." Same-day appointments for patients in need. An electronic system for tracking whether patients meet their personal health goals over time. Group meetings to review the patients scheduled for that day, attended by the entire medical staff: two doctors, two nurses, the receptionist, the social worker, and eight "health coaches" who see patients most frequently of all, working with them in person, by phone, and by email to help them follow their treatment plans and prevent future illnesses. When the clinic has a day that none of its patients is in a hospital, the staff celebrates. And while this approach is still new and not fully proven, the medical costs of the patients who visit the Special Care Center have dropped 25 percent.

This success could be a textbook example of how to clear out greedy bastards and create a more productive system. Concentrating resources on the hot spots provided the visibility. For the first time, doctors could see where ineffective care and excessive spending were taking place, and use digital technology to help plan an alternative. The Special Care Center offered patients a meaningful choice, a practical alternative to traditional doctor offices and hospitals. The new approaches to payment and staffing—especially the financial arrangements that reward collaboration, and those eight health coaches charged with helping to prevent disease—aligned the interests of the doctors and the patients. The result was healthier outcomes at a price closer to the true cost.

Will this approach work on a large scale? Denmark has seen comparable results nationwide. When the country improved primary care services—for example, by paying doctors to respond to patient email and paying nurses to manage the care of patients with complex needs—hospital use declined so much that fewer facilities were needed. Twenty years ago, Denmark had over 150 hospitals for its five million people. Now it has about 70, and the number is still shrinking.

Can Doctors Prosper While Working as a Team for Health?

But you don't have to go to Denmark. In the winter of 2011, I took my television show to the Mayo Clinic in Rochester, Minnesota. Mayo has been near the top of *U.S. News & World Report*'s Best Hospitals rankings for twenty years. It can seem a kind of miracle. Not only is the clinic a world leader in many fields, with doctors collaborating to improve procedures, technologies, and patient outcomes, but also its world-class care is twice as efficient as other clinics and hospitals in the area. One study found that the medical care for elderly Medicare patients in the last, most expensive years of life cost roughly half at Mayo than at nearby providers.

In Rochester, I interviewed Dr. Kevin Bennet, chief of engineering, who explained how the Mayo Clinic approach has challenged the conventional practice of medicine from the time of its founding in 1889. Dr. William Worrall Mayo, who'd studied medicine in Europe, sent his two sons to different American medical schools and continued to practice alongside them. Ordinarily, at that time, every doctor was expected to set up shop in a different town, giving him a little monopoly of his own. But all three Mayos chose to stay and practice in Rochester, so that family dinners provided opportunities for the three physicians to discuss their patients. Because each had different training and experience, they'd compare different approaches and discovered which ones worked best. As Bennet told me, "All of a sudden, you had a nucleus of a culture that says, 'Let's do the experiment, let's understand, let's compare, and then let's select the process/procedure that works best for our patients." This is now known as the multidisciplinary approach, or multidisciplinary care.

With three doctors in one practice, one could travel and study while the others looked after their patients, and then the traveler could return and share what he had learned. In Europe, one visiting Mayo learned from famed British surgeon Joseph Lister how to use carbolic acid to kill germs, making it possible to perform surgery without causing infections. In Boston, a visiting Mayo saw a demonstration of ether used as anesthesia—a considerable improvement over managing the pain of surgery by having the patient drink rum and bite down on a leather belt. They brought these techniques back to their hospital and combined them. "For the first time in history," Bennet told me, "you could have an operation, you didn't feel it, and you lived."

Today a patient at the Mayo Clinic receives a similarly customized approach. He or she has one doctor, but that doctor's role is to act like a musical conductor, orchestrating all the physicians and other hospital staff the patient will see. Time for consultations with other members of a patient's "orchestra" is scheduled into everyone's day. In addition to the medical division, the hospital has an engineering division that can customize medical devices for the patient or for the doctors. For example, when Mayo physicians were preparing to separate conjoined Siamese twins who shared a liver, the engineering department constructed a full-size replica of the organ, so that the medical team could sit together and discuss options until they agreed exactly how to divide it in half, cut by cut, in order to leave each twin with a functioning liver.

Each patient at Mayo receives the benefit of group problem solving like this, but the members of the patient's orchestra play together only because the hospital staff's incentives have been aligned with those of their patients. The conventional fee-for-service doctor, remember, receives a fee every time he performs an exam or orders a procedure, and he gets the biggest fees for the procedures he performs in his own office with his own equipment. If that conventional doctor were asked to sit in on a group problem-solving session in the Mayo style, he would do so knowing that he would earn little or nothing for his time. Likewise, if he was asked to share his expertise so that engineers outside of his office could make the perfect medical technology for a given patient, he would earn little or nothing. Every time he tried to use the Mayo approach, it would cost him money, because the time he spent on innovative group problem solving would take away from time back in his office, performing lucrative exams and procedures.

As Kevin Bennet explained, for a patient-centered approach like Mayo's to work, "You need a core group of medical professionals that can work well together, that will show up at meetings, that will communicate"—and who know that "if they come to a meeting . . . it does not impact their personal income." For this reason, Mayo pays its doctors a fixed salary, freeing them to focus on providing great care, not maximizing the number of fees they can collect. Mayo has an admirable culture of innovation and service, but that culture is made possible by financial incentives that reward quality patient care, not quantity of procedures sold.

Surely these are isolated examples, right? Can this really be scaled up to serve everyone in the United States, and can we possibly transition from our current broken model to one that works? Yes. According to Phillip Longman of *Washington Monthly* magazine, we've already done it, at least for veterans. In the 1970s and 1980s, the US Veterans Health Administration was notorious for its dirty hospitals and scandalous conditions, grimly depicted in movies such as *Born on the Fourth of July*. In 2003, after a serious reform effort, Veterans health facilities surpassed traditional Medicare fee-for-service on eleven out of eleven measures of quality. It outdid conventional managed care systems in treating diabetes on seven out of seven measures. In fact, the National Committee for Quality Assurance found that the VHA system beat the Mayo Clinic in quality of care! And in 2010, despite severe budget constraints, it served 8.3 million Americans during 75.6 million outpatient visits. It's a big system.

In the 1990s, Longman writes, physician Kenneth Kizer was put in charge and immediately began shaking up the VA bureaucracy. He instituted a number of reforms that align incentives. The VHA already had the advantage we've seen with the Mayo Clinic, in that doctors are salaried instead of charging a fee-for-service. Its physicians don't clamor for expensive technology just because it boosts profits; they are paid to treat people, period. Kizer changed the culture dramatically, taking advantage of these natural benefits. The VHA began focusing less on delivering acute hospital care and more on primary care and outpatient services, a more efficient allocation of resources. To reduce medical errors, it put in place a medical data sharing system that kept patient histories and prevented dangerous drug interactions and other treatment combinations. This had the beneficial effect of radically reducing paperwork for doctors and patients. The system was so good that the VHA offered its software free on the Internet, and it has been downloaded and used all over the world.

Just not in America. According to Longman, doctors in private practice and other hospitals refused to use the software because they lack a financial incentive to invest in electronic medical records and other improvements to the quality of the care they offer. Improvements in the VHA came from a relentless focus on quality. Some are so obvious that they make you scream in frustration: such as noting that a surgeon operates on the wrong limb one out of every fifteen thousand times. This is not because the surgeon got the limbs mixed up. As Longman described in his *Washington Monthly* article, the VHA found "that about a third of time . . . the surgeon is not operating on the patient he thinks he is." The VHA system eliminated errors like this, while the for-profit sector did not. Sometimes it's just not profitable enough to make sure that you're operating on the right limb—or even the right patient! I guess we can consider my friend Larry lucky that he kept all of his extremities.

The VHA system has one other advantage that even the Mayo Clinic does not: it keeps its patients for life. This means that investing in reducing long-term medical expenses, twenty or thirty years out, makes financial sense. A for-profit health insurance company does not care if you get sick in ten years, because by then you will most likely be a competitor's problem. Furthermore, the Veterans Health Administration can manage its information systemwide—

with millions of patients, it has a powerful database that can identify best practices and common vulnerabilities across patients. This is health care done right.

Optimize the Patient Experience

Around the country, evidence already exists that aligning doctors' financial incentives with their patients' needs makes them more effective. Gardiner Harris reported in the *New York Times* that as more doctors take salaried jobs in hospitals rather than run solo practices, and as more women become physicians, their political and personal efforts have shifted from protecting their position as business owners to protecting public health. This trend has been observed in states as diverse as Maine, Arizona, South Dakota, and Oregon. Harris profiled one example: Dr. Lee Thibodeau, a self-described conservative from Oregon who once paid nearly $85,000 a year for malpractice insurance and "was among the most politically active doctors in the state on the issue of liability. Then, in 2006, he sold his practice, took a job with a local health care system, stopped paying the insurance premiums, and ended his advocacy on the issue. 'It's not my priority anymore,' Dr. Thibodeau said." His new priority? "To optimize the patient experience."

That is a daunting task, when the interests of the players are out of alignment and we get lost in the bogus political distractions that are so helpful to greedy bastards fighting to preserve their interests at everyone else's expense. Take the Medicare debate. Republicans want to replace the current system, in which the federal government pays claims, with block grants from individual states, limiting the total payments from the government and obligating individuals to pay the rest. The Democrats treat the current payment system like a holy relic that can't be touched. Enormous amounts of time, money, and attention have been devoted to this argument, but it misses the bigger problem.

If the goal is to incentivize Mayo-style health professionals and hot-spotting patients to work with aligned interests to preserve health actively, the system of payments has to support that goal. That's why the VA works. But as Joe Wiesenthal pointed out on Business Insider, health care in America has become so expensive and continues to grow so fast that it will overwhelm our economy *no matter who pays for it or how they pay*. Economist Dean Baker of the Center for Economic and Policy Research explained on *Radio Free Dylan*, "It's not that [Medicare and Medicaid] are inefficient. They're actually somewhat more efficient than their private-sector counterparts. It's simply that health care is unaffordable." Unless we can stop the greedy bastards in health care from endlessly driving up the cost of care, no payment system, new or old, will matter.

Both private insurance and government-funded coverage treat disease but do not promote health. But if we spend our health care money directly with multidisciplinary, targeted physician teams and health coaches, the system creates a naturally occurring incentive, transaction by transaction, to reward those who nurture health. We know it works, both here and abroad, as we've seen with the VHA.

Didn't We Just Reform Health Care?

But wait. Didn't the Health Care Reform Bill signed into law in 2010 make any difference? To be fair, it did. President Obama and the Democrats got two things right.

First, they collected many strong cost-cutting ideas, including several I've discussed here, that are scheduled to be implemented in the coming years. For example, the government will begin paying some hospitals to implement cost-cutting measures. Those that succeed get to keep some of the money they save. Those that fail have to return their payments.

Second, Obama mandated coverage for all Americans. This may prove to be a huge moral victory, and potentially a highly practical one, since any kind of insurance is most affordable when everyone buys in. But the economic benefits of the mandate will never be seen because the Democrats were recklessly negligent in addressing costs. They have allowed the vampire to keep its teeth in our neck and all the little greedy-bastard monopolies to remain in place. They pushed everyone into the least efficient system: the private employer-based health insurance market.

That means that each of the millions of new patients required to buy health insurance is also required to pay the price-inflated doctors, the bureaucratic monster, the drug extortionists, the insurance price fixers, and so on. The best possible world for greedy bastards is when the government can legally require people to pay fixed prices, and that is what Obama's health care reform has done. Democrats, I know, will say that they did the best they could, but it is not good enough. "It's a bigger bailout for the insurance industry than AIG," Howard Dean told *Good Morning America*.

Republicans will say that these flaws are reason enough to tear down the entire system, but they too are just caving to the greedy bastards: if "Obamacare" is repealed, it will end many valuable approaches to cost cutting that could weaken the vampire's grip over time.

Once again, in the health insurance debate, we find the politicians stuck in a circuitous, wrongheaded, and distracting debate. Republicans cry "Free market!" and liberals try to get the government to do what the free market can't. But what if neither the free market nor the government can give us the kind of system we need? Government-controlled health care can cover everyone, as it does in England, but there are long waits for many procedures, and the government decides your treatment options. A study in the journal *Health Affairs* found that only 25 percent of British citizens were happy with their government-controlled system. That may be more than the 17 percent of Americans who are happy with employer-based insurance, but not by much. Earlier I talked up the advantages of the VHA, but that kind of system requires strong leadership and a commitment to excellence. We are fortunate to have it in the VHA now, but the legacy of poor quality care is too powerful to ignore. I'm not comfortable putting everyone's health care in one basket, for fear that it will look like the 1970s' VHA, and not today's.

So what choice is left if you want to do better than free-market American-style health insurance *and* government-controlled British-style health insurance? One system would free patients to make their own choices—you and your doctor choose what's best for you—but still cover everyone. How could that work? Either you have to give them unlimited government money or somehow guarantee that every citizen has enough money to pay for his or her health care. But where would the money come from, if not the government?

Economist Tim Harford points to Singapore's care system, which both requires universal participation and addresses the cost to government. First, you are required to buy a policy to cover the kinds of catastrophes that result in very costly claims: car accidents, cancer, and so on. But because such catastrophes are relatively rare and because everyone is required to have a policy, the policies are cheap. Second, you contribute to a health care savings account yearly, from birth, and use that savings account to pay for your own routine medical expenses. Most people have the bulk of their medical expenses later in life, so by the time they need most of the money, they have already saved tens of thousands of dollars to build up a reserve. (For those too poor to make full contributions to their savings accounts, the government makes up the difference.) If they don't spend all of their health savings, they can leave the account to others, such as a spouse or children. The money comes from individuals rather than from the government, and decisions about how it is spent are made mostly by those individuals themselves—not by the government and not by a company claims adjuster.

Singapore's system addresses the two structural obstacles to an optimal health care system. First, no amount of spending on disease care will, in itself, create health—and what we need, therefore, is to create incentives to spend on prevention. Second, when it comes to health care, the market will never align our personal interests with our national interests, because everyone will be tempted, economically, to avoid paying into the system when they are younger and healthier, and then to ask for more care than they paid for when they are older and in greater need.

So is Singapore the answer? The answer is to break the grip of the special interests, to learn what has worked around the world and on a small scale in this country, and to test practical solutions until we find what will work to kill the vampire and realign the health care system around health—no matter who comes up with the idea.

5

The Castle Is Collapsing

Imagine that I offered you the chance to go into business with me. Here's the deal: we assist in the sale of a highly desirable product. So desirable, in fact, that most Americans believe they can't live without it. Our business is to loan the buyer the money to buy the product, with an average loan of $24,000. What's special about this business is that it can't fail, because our buyers can't renege on their loans. Even if they declare bankruptcy, they still owe us. They face a life-

time of damaged credit histories, and they may have their wages and tax refunds seized by the government, but we get one hundred cents on the dollar. Their employment and other choices may be impacted for decades, and their ability to compete in the global economy will likely suffer, but never mind. The best part, though, for us is that if they truly can't pay, the government will pay us instead. We can't lose.

Sounds like the kind of business only a greedy bastard could love, doesn't it? And the kind of deal that most of us, as customers, wouldn't go near. The sort of scam you'd warn your friends and children about. Except that the majority of customers *are* children; teenagers with little understanding of what effect these loans may have on their lives. I'm describing the college loan market, which has become a big greedy-bastard business. As of June 2010, the total value of student loans, reports the website FinAid, approached $1 trillion. According to the Federal Reserve, that's more than enough money to pay off every credit card held by every single person in the country.

Prices for education have spiraled out of control. Inflation in higher education over the past thirty years, according to *The Economist,* has been two and a half times the rate of normal inflation, which puts it even higher than inflation for health care. According to NPR's *Planet Money* podcast and blog, there are some good reasons for these rising costs. For one thing, colleges must hire educated "workers" to provide their "services," and educated workers are increasingly expensive. Technology has not (yet) led to cost reductions in education the way it has in, say, manufacturing. But the second, larger problem is that educational institutions are in a position to charge more or less whatever they want. "Academic inflation makes medical inflation look modest by comparison," *The Economist* reported.

Demand continues to grow because a college education is now widely considered a necessity for success. As President Obama told his first joint session of Congress, "Education is no longer a pathway to opportunity, it is a prerequisite." Many students and their parents believe they must do whatever is required to earn a college degree. At the same time, colleges don't compete on price. As *The Economist* explained, "The big problem is that high-status institutions such as universities tend to compete with each other on academic reputation (which is enhanced by star professors) and bling (luxurious dormitories and fancy sports stadiums) rather than value for money. This starts at the top: Yale would never dream of competing with Harvard on price." Where Harvard and Yale lead, many have followed, focusing resources on creating an aura of prestige rather than on student learning. *The Chronicle of Higher Education*, a magazine for college faculty, administrators, and students, described "an arms race of expenditures triggered by the pursuit of prestige." (Similar pressures are at work in private elementary and high schools. The *New York Times* reported that tuition at private New York City schools had risen 79 percent in only ten years, now topping $40,000 a year.)

Prices might not rise so fast if there were price resistance from the buyers, but they get hit with the classic Very Bad Deal. "We're going to give you something you want at what seems like a great price today, thanks to our influence with the federal government. You won't feel the real costs until later." The result is what Tamara Draut, author of *Strapped: Why America's 20- and 30-Somethings Can't Get Ahead*, calls a "debt-for-diploma system." You go into debt, you get a diploma. Doesn't the diploma guarantee earning power that more than offsets the debt? Not anymore. The diploma makes an enormous difference for those who can get hired, but many graduates can't get a job that makes use of their degree. According to the US Bureau of Labor Statistics, from 2000 to mid-2008, there was an average of about two unemployed Americans for every job opening. But from mid-2008 to mid-2011, the average was over five unemployed for every job opening.

The end result, Draut told me, is that "we have a whole generation twenty-four thousand dollars in debt. . . . They have graduated, but nobody will hire them. They're back at home in their childhood bedroom." So what does a college education mean? Is it a wise investment in a young person's future, or is it just an expensive gamble, a multi-thousand-dollar lottery ticket that only profits the banksters?

The fastest-growing piece of the higher education business is for-profit universities such as the University of Phoenix, which are also the biggest recipients of federal subsidies. For-profits educate 12 percent of students, according to the *Chronicle of Higher Education,* but they receive one-fourth of all student aid and account for half the student loans in default. More than one in seven students at a for-profit school will fail to pay their loans in the first two years. To put that another way, for-profits take in twice as much government money as other colleges, yet they get that bigger cut by "awarding" loan packages to students who won't be able to pay them back. As Education Secretary Arne Duncan said in a press release, the worst of the for-profit colleges are "saddling students with debt they cannot afford in exchange for degrees and certificates they cannot use." The students wind up broke, we taxpayers have to cover their loans, and the for-profit colleges become the hot growth area in education—

but only because of taxpayer money. "Federal dollars," according to the *Chronicle*, "totaled 87 percent of revenue at 14 for-profit schools in 2009, including the largest, the University of Phoenix."

How do I know that the for-profit debt-for-diploma system is a classic vampire industry scam, using political influence to pocket taxpayer money? I followed the money trail when the system was challenged. The Obama administration tried to impose a rule that would end federally guaranteed loans for schools with records of burdening students with high debt and low job prospects. In response, the for-profit colleges set up the Coalition for Educational Success, a lobbying group that would represent the for-profit colleges and the companies that own them. It hired former Pennsylvania governor Ed Rendell and former New Jersey governor Tom Kean as advisers to formulate new codes of conduct to, as CES put it, "improve and ensure transparency, disclosure, training, [and] provide strong new protections for students" attending "career colleges." Also brought on as consultants? Former Rhode Island Attorney General Patrick C. Lynch, former staffers at the Department of Education, and fourteen ex-congressmen.

In all, the coalition spent $8 million on lobbying in 2010 alone, and $2 million in campaign contributions. And it won. Over three hundred members of Congress threatened to defund the Department of Education's regulatory apparatus if the proposed rule to cut off loans was implemented. Threatened with losing its funding, the DOE substantially weakened the rule. Barmak Nassirian, who heads a trade association of nonprofit college admissions officers, told the magazine *American Prospect*, "What we see here is that the for-profit school industry has not just bought off the Republican Party but has done an amazing job of buying off the elite of the political left as well."

I would like to see VICI values applied to the education industry. We could begin with visibility and price integrity. Don't students and their parents, like patients in the health care system, deserve to see an itemized bill? Not just a list of what they receive—course credits, room, board—but what their tuition covers. How much goes to management salaries, how much goes to fancy new buildings? How much goes to teaching? Every college should be forced to disclose its spending in an ongoing web-based audit, and spending decisions should be a factor in the national rankings of schools so that students and parents can see whether the school's interests align with their own needs. As Andrew Jenks, filmmaker, MTV host and New York University dropout told me in a private interview, "If there was an ongoing web-based audit, then you could see a school's true priorities: Is NYU trying to take over the world or teach its students? If you could see what the institutions were spending money on, you'd have a much better idea of where you'd want to go to school."

Real Estate–Based Education

Elementary and high school funding is a racket as well. There is no other country in the world that funds its public schools the way we do. As founder of the MIT Media Laboratory Nicholas Negroponte told me, "When you tell somebody from a foreign country that you come from someplace whose school system is based on real estate taxes, they look at you as if you come from a different planet." We have nineteen thousand separate but unequal school systems.

The current system takes hot-spotting, which you read about in chapter 4 on health care, and reverses it. The real estate–based education system overfunds the few wealthy schools (which need funding the least) while reducing resources for those most in need, maximizing the harm done. For proof, consider that just two thousand high schools in our country produce 50 percent of all dropouts, according to the policy and advocacy organization Alliance for Excellent Education. This reverse hot-spotting creates "dropout factories" (mostly made up of minorities) where the graduating class contains on average only 60 percent of those who'd entered as freshman.

The misdirection of education money parallels the perverse misalignment of interests that we saw in the health care industry, where we pay for bureaucracy and disease treatments, when what we actually want is improved health. In education, we pay crippling amounts of money for expensive buildings, over-the-top athletic programs, high administrative salaries, frequent testing, and teacher job security rather than what we need: improved learning.

A Harness of Debt

Parents struggle to avoid the inferior schools, leading to bankster-funded bidding wars for housing in better school districts. As Elizabeth Warren and Amelia Tyagi described in *The Two-Income Trap*, in some districts where new, well-funded public schools have been built, average home prices have tripled within a few years. Even the addition of a second parent's income is not enough to keep up with the resulting price inflation. "In their desperate rush to save their children from failing schools," Warren and Tyagi wrote, "families are literally spending themselves into bankruptcy." To do so, they must rely on a real estate loan market run amok on government-sponsored credit. The cycle repeats when children go to college: according to Warren and Tyagi, each year one million parents take out second mortgages on their homes to pay college costs. At every step, banksters are taking a cut of the money spent chasing a good education—and distorting our choices.

Once the schools get their real estate–based funding, their spending priorities are strange. Compared with other OECD nations, American schools spend far more on the parts of schools that have nothing to do with classroom teaching. A 2002 state-sponsored report by Standard & Poor's in Michigan found that "from 1997 to 1999, while the total amount of education spending in Michigan increased nearly 7 percent, central administration spending increased approximately 18 percent." In 2011, New Jersey imposed a cap on superintendent salaries based on the number of students supervised, while Indiana considered such a cap but did not pass it. Similar battles are being waged in states across the country.

Beyond nonteaching administrators, we also lavish education money on capital investments, school buildings, renovations, and compensation for nonteaching staff such as principals in pursuit of prestige, not necessarily learning. Compared with South Korea, for example, we spend far more on buildings and far less on keeping class size manageable and making sure that teachers have ample time for lesson planning. We collect funding for public education based on real estate and then use that "education" money to build still more real estate.

The end results are that greedy bastards profit from new participants in the college loan and real estate debt markets, while we trap capital that might be more productive elsewhere in the housing and student financing markets. Parents and college graduates alike wind up in a harness of debt, unable to follow opportunity around the country as Americans have traditionally done, and as our economy needs us to do in order for talent to find its most valuable expression. To find jobs that will repay their debts, many of our best and brightest choose to work in the vampire industries that put them in the debt harness. It's a greedy-bastard brain drain.

The vampire education industry has exacerbated the damage already done to social mobility by vampire banking and health care industries. As documented by Equality Trust, a British group that works to reduce income inequality, although the United States is known as the land of opportunity, the children of the rich in America are now most likely to stay rich, and the children of poor are most likely to stay poor, compared with children in six European countries and Canada.

The Castle and the Ocean

To be fair, education is not thoroughly under the control of greedy bastards, and the amount of waste and theft is far smaller than what you find in the other industries discussed in this book. But like any vampire industry, education increasingly gives its customers an inefficient product that doesn't suit its present needs. As a percentage of our GDP, we spend the second most of any developed country (only Iceland spends more) but when it comes to high school graduation rates, we're nineteenth in the world. For college graduates, we're fifteenth.

However you measure it, the decline has been steep. As bankster-turned-philanthropist Mike Milken told me, in 1960

Americans were the best-educated people in the world. The average adult had two more years of education than the average in any other country. Now many other regions have equaled or surpassed us. Some of the leaders in reading, science, and math are in Shanghai, Korea, and Finland, according to scores from the Program for International Student Assessment (PISA), a series of academic tests administered to fifteen-year-olds from around the world every three years through the multinational Organization for Economic Cooperation and Development (OECD). The United States comes in seventeenth in reading, twenty-third in science, and thirty-first in math. David Banks, founder of the Eagle Academy for Young Men, an all-boys public high school in New York City, likes to say that the only measure on which American students are still number one is self-esteem. Even as we fall further behind, we still believe we're winning. This gap is a sign that all of our investment in prestige over learning is having the desired effect—just not the one we all want.

The harm to American students is a theft and a shame, but this failure goes beyond education. We need education to prepare every industry to meet the challenges of the digital age with its accelerating rate of change. Education may be a small part of the entirety of American society, but it's small in the way that motor oil is a small part of a car. If we don't have it, we don't keep the engine lubricated with a social culture of learning, the engine of our society seizes up, and the entire vehicle breaks down. I've spoken to CEOs of the many great manufacturers in this country, and I hear repeatedly their frustration at not finding sufficient numbers of qualified candidates to work in their industries. And when almost anyone with a computer and a cell phone can conduct business with anyone else, anywhere, we need an educational system that prepares us to adapt to fast, ongoing change.

All major industries face steep and disorienting change, and they're all looking to education to meet these new challenges. The breadth and depth of these changes are immense. It is as if for thousands of years, we have lived in a castle: tall, solid, reliable. Those who knew their way around the castle had the power. They could keep out the people they didn't want to come in, as well as control the flow of information. But now technology disrupts our lives with increasing speed, like waves. We're realizing that, all along, the castle was made of sandstone and that the digital revolution is a series of waves that will wash it into the ocean.

In the past few years, we've felt the castle start to buckle. Panicked greedy bastards convince the government to reinforce their rigid systems with a loophole here and a bailout there. It works for a while, but in the long run, we as a society need to help people learn to stop clinging to the old model of living in a castle and start building better boats for our new life on the open water. We need an educational system that's going to help us thrive in this changing environment.

To put it another way, vampire industries are bleeding us dry of capital, but capital is not just money. Capital refers to anything valuable in creating new ventures. I asked John Hennessy, president of Stanford University, how Stanford came to be involved in creating innovative companies such as Sun Microsystems, Yahoo!, Google, and so many others. He pointed to the fact that from the engineering quadrangle at Stanford, it's only a fifteen-minute walk to the closest venture capitalist; the people who have the capital are right next to the human capital of the students who are inventing the twenty-first century. The ideas, the vision, the relation-ships, and what Hennessy called the "youthful exuberance" of his students are as important as the checks that venture capitalists can write.

But when our education system maintains an outdated status quo because it is profitable for the greedy bastards, that status quo chokes our human capital, threatening our ability to compete not just in education but also in every area. Frank Moss, director of the Massachusetts Institute of Technology Media Lab, told me, "It's the system that's broken. I have no doubt that Americans in many ways are the most innovative and creative people in the world, but if the system doesn't encourage them to take risks, then that innovation, that creativity will eventually be beaten out of us."

Sounds nasty, doesn't it? So follow me now on the educational path from birth onward. You'll find that there are amazing new methods for more effective and valuable learning; ripe opportunities to nourish the human capital we need for this country to compete and thrive. Realizing these opportunities, though, is going to chal-lenge our ideas of what good schooling is—and threaten the greedy bastards at every level.

Begin When Learning Begins

We may still think of education as beginning on the first day of kindergarten, but by then our children have already been learning for roughly five years. Our country's educational policies, programs, and practices typically don't take this learning seriously. As Daniel Pedersen, founding president of the Buffett Early Childhood Fund, remarked to me, "We would never have designed the public education system we have now in the way it now works if we [knew] what we know now about how the brain grows and develops."

Specifically, we now know that in children under three, seven hundred brain synapses are formed each second, creating the ability to process their senses, use language, and develop their vocabulary as well as their reasoning skills. The architecture of the brain—the way these synapses are connected—is determined by what Hirokazu Yoshikawa, professor of education at Harvard, calls "serve and return" interaction. When a toddler does or says something, it's like a tennis player serving a ball over the net. If someone else responds meaningfully, hitting the ball back, the game continues, and the brain connections are made as the toddler develops knowledge and skills. But if no one returns the serve, the synapses keep forming, but they are not organized for communicating and learning—a prerequisite for effective problem solving. As a result, by the age of only *eighteen months*, there is an observable difference in learning between those who get the chance to use those developing synapses early on, especially with adults who talk and read and explore the world with them, and those who don't.

Susie Buffett, of the Buffett Early Childhood Fund, explained it to me this way: "When a child takes the CAT test in first grade, and there's a question about a giraffe or an elephant, and they've been growing up in a home with no books, no *Sesame Street*, no Discovery Channel, no trip to the zoo—with very little language that isn't negative—the child takes the test, and they don't know what the giraffe or the elephant is, and that's where they start failing." That child lacks the basic context for understanding that a child with a fuller early learning environment gets, and he or she will be playing catch-up from age three on. As economics professor James J.

Heckman has shown in a study, once those gaps develop, there is little anyone can do to close them.

As a result, Kevin Drum wrote in *Mother Jones* magazine, we would do much better to expose small children to programs such as Early Head Start than try to make up for lost time later. "Intensive, early interventions, by contrast [to later efforts], genuinely seem to work," Drum concluded. "They produce children who learn better, develop critical life skills, have fewer problems in childhood and adolescence, commit fewer crimes, earn more money, and just generally live happier, more stable, and more productive lives. If we spent $50 billion less on K-12 education—in both public and private money—and instead spent $50 billion more on early intervention programs, we'd almost certainly get a way bigger bang for the buck."

A report by the nonprofit public policy organization the Brookings Institution observed that of ten federal social programs evaluated since 1990, only one showed "meaningful . . . positive effects." That program was Early Head Start (EHS), a federally funded, community-based program for low-income families with infants and toddlers and pregnant women. However, as Susie Buffett told me, due to budget limitations only 6 percent of the children the government defines as eligible for EHS were enrolled in the program—and the level of funding to maintain that may not be sustained in future budgets. When it comes to boosting learning and achievement for young Americans, we know the problem: intelligence and talent are equally distributed through all populations, but the natural equality between poor and rich is undermined by the selective opportunity to develop that intelligence and talent. We also know what would solve the problem; we just aren't doing it. But perhaps that is no surprise.

Education

Every choice to align the interests of teachers and taxpayers with everyone else through proven group- and web-based problem solving methods enhances all problem-solving; every choice to breach it destroys it.

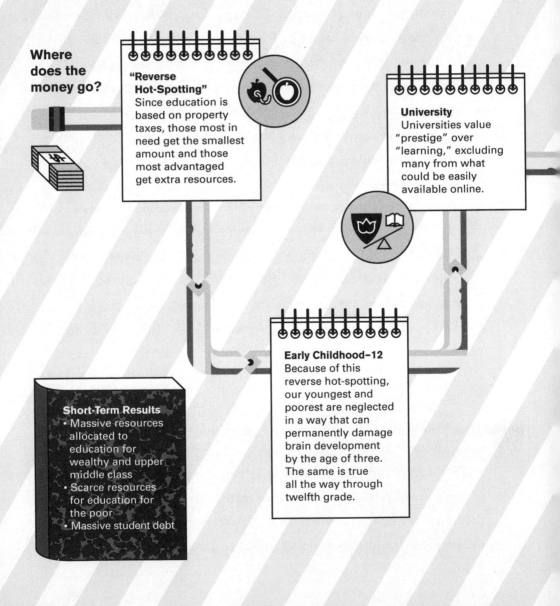

Where does the money go?

"Reverse Hot-Spotting"
Since education is based on property taxes, those most in need get the smallest amount and those most advantaged get extra resources.

University
Universities value "prestige" over "learning," excluding many from what could be easily available online.

Early Childhood–12
Because of this reverse hot-spotting, our youngest and poorest are neglected in a way that can permanently damage brain development by the age of three. The same is true all the way through twelfth grade.

Short-Term Results
• Massive resources allocated to education for wealthy and upper middle class
• Scarce resources for education for the poor
• Massive student debt

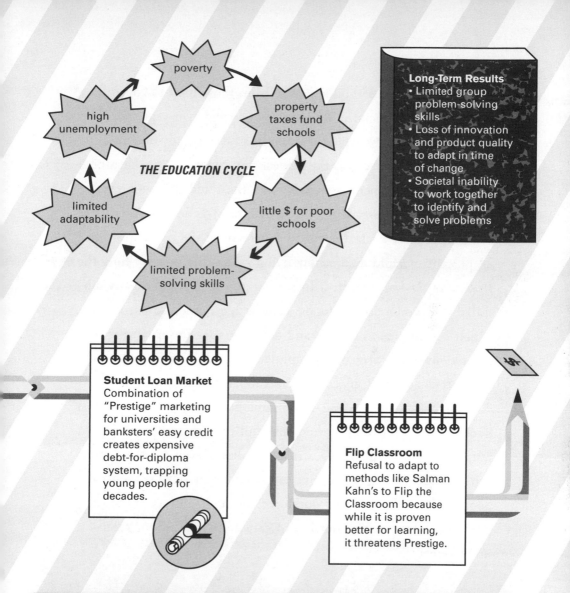

THE EDUCATION CYCLE

- poverty
- property taxes fund schools
- little $ for poor schools
- limited problem-solving skills
- limited adaptability
- high unemployment

Long-Term Results
- Limited group problem-solving skills
- Loss of innovation and product quality to adapt in time of change
- Societal inability to work together to identify and solve problems

Student Loan Market
Combination of "Prestige" marketing for universities and banksters' easy credit creates expensive debt-for-diploma system, trapping young people for decades.

Flip Classroom
Refusal to adapt to methods like Salman Kahn's to Flip the Classroom because while it is proven better for learning, it threatens Prestige.

THE FIX

1 End "reverse hot-spotting." Since education is based on property taxes, those most in need get the smallest amount and those most advantaged get extra resources. Fund education through a national tax structure and use hot-spotting to directly address worst areas.

2 Same as Fix 1. See Susie Buffett and Early Childhood Foundation.

3/4 Universities value "prestige" over "learning," excluding many from what could be easily available online. Adopt methods like Salman Kahn's to Flip the Classroom because it is proven better for learning right through university level.

5 Demand visibility for all university spending and refuse to pay to go to schools that sell prestige over learning.

If we were to shift $50 billion away from those used to controlling that money and spend it instead on one- and two-year-olds who don't vote or shop, we would disappoint a lot of greedy bastards.

Ultimately, poverty is the biggest root cause of our educational gap. As unemployment rises, driven by the trade and bank extraction, poverty increases with it. In 2010, the fraction of Americans living in poverty clicked up to 15.1 percent of the population, and 22 percent of children are now living below the poverty line, the *Wall Street Journal* reported. In the same way that politicians subsidize the production of foods such as high-fructose corn syrup, which contributes to obesity and diabetes, they incentivize wealth extractions—resulting in unemployment and a spike in poverty, which then adversely affect our educational system.

Making matters worse, those same poor children are the most likely to end up eating a heavy diet full of corn syrup—and poor nutrition and learning are inextricably linked as well. It's the American poverty double whammy: impaired brain development and poor nutrition. It hurts our workforce and limits our ability to solve problems, while spiking our health care costs. Talk about room for improvement!

Flip the Classroom Upside Down

Once we give kids the best chance possible for early development, how do we prepare them for a world more like an ocean than a castle? Traditional education had three basic components: the teacher lectures, students take notes and study what they're taught, and then the teacher tests the students on what they have retained. Their test scores measure their success.

That approach made perfect sense when two things were true: First, that the teachers already knew what the kids would need to know, because the rate of change in society and the world at large was relatively slow. Second, that the best technologies available were old reliables such as blackboard and chalk, pen and paper, printed books, and paper exams. But as the castle collapses, we need to ask, how can we best learn, and what are the best means to teach? To me this is the most important point. Successful problem solving comes from VICI values. It's true of the health clinics I described in chapter 4, where multidisciplinary teams meet to figure out what makes the most sense for each patient. It's true of a factory that has to adapt to fluctuations in demand, coordinating with designers, suppliers, and shippers who may be scattered around the world, to figure out on the fly how best to meet its customers' needs. It's true of how my team creates our news program, as we try to meet the evolving needs of our viewers. In all these cases, success comes from a variety of people with different skills communicating openly to align their interests and make the best possible choices as a group toward a mutually shared goal.

That's more than a skill. It also takes passion and enthusiasm for the hard work required: problem solvers do best when they enjoy their work. As founder of the MIT Media Laboratory Nicholas Negroponte told me, "If we look at what constitutes learning, it's basically about passion." The danger here is that traditional education not only fails to give our students the skills they need but also can kill their passion. "If I do very well on a test score where you're testing me on what I memorized," says Negroponte, "not only do I not necessarily become part of a creative society, you may have already whipped it out of me. So I'll learn math, but I'll hate mathematics.

I'll learn geography names but hate understanding what the planet looks like. That's what has to change."

One practical example of teaching to encourage group-based problem solving is STEM schools, an acronym for science, technology, engineering, and mathematics. In STEM schools such as Cleveland High in Seattle, the theory is that textbook learning is never enough. Real learning takes place when groups of students work together on real-life projects. One key part of STEM education is partnering with community organizations, giving students a glimpse into the "real world" and providing them mentors and internships, while building relationships with companies that the students might work for someday, keeping the talent local.

Even as the goal of education moves toward group-based problem solving rather than individual success on tests, there will always be a need for students to master traditional knowledge. But technology has created new possibilities for acquiring that knowledge, many of which are still being discovered. Salman Khan was a hedge fund analyst in New York who occasionally tutored his cousins when he visited them in New Orleans. He put some of his lessons on YouTube, so that the boys could review them when he was away. To his surprise, they told him they preferred to have him explaining math in a video rather than in person. As Khan described at an annual TED conference, "At first, it's very unintuitive, but when you actually think about it from their point of view, it makes a ton of sense. You have this situation where now they can pause and repeat their cousin, without feeling like they're wasting my time. If they have to review something that they should have learned a couple of weeks ago, or maybe a couple of years ago, they don't have to be embarrassed and ask their cousin. They can just watch those videos." The technology let him conform his teaching to suit their needs as learners rather than modify their style of learning to his lesson.

Khan began receiving compliments from other YouTube users who'd discovered his videos, saying that watching him online had enabled them to understand concepts that had eluded them in regular classrooms. They were also enjoying it more. As one calculus student wrote, "This was the first time I smiled doing a derivative." Then some teachers wrote to say that they used the videos to "flip the classroom." Viewing video lectures was now assigned as homework, and what used to be homework was done in the classroom, with the teachers available to answer questions.

As this approach developed further, in the Los Altos, California, school district and elsewhere, lectures were shown on video, and tests were administered and graded by computer. Teachers, who spent less time lecturing and grading, had much more time to work with students in areas where they needed extra help. Technology did not replace the teachers, it freed them to address individual students' needs. The data from the computerized testing showed teachers exactly what areas were most challenging for students—the educational hot-spots in the class—and they would use class time to work with them one on one or pair up a student struggling in a certain area with a peer tutor who had already found his or her way.

Video lectures might be equally valuable at the college level. One president of an American university suggested to me that a much more effective system would combine Web videos of the best lecturers in America with teacher-led problem solving in class. This would expand the impact of America's best professors and let strong researchers who were mediocre classroom teachers pursue innovative research instead. But it represents a huge threat to the status quo.

Encourage Mistakes, Expect Mastery

Traditional teaching awards a grade and then moves on. If a student gets an 85 on a test, he or she has a solid B, but that student has missed 15 percent of the material. Those gaps—"Swiss cheese holes in your knowledge," Khan calls them—may prove costly later. So instead of giving students a grade for a unit and then moving on, the online Khan Academy and its partner schools ask students to keep studying a unit until they can answer ten questions correctly in a row. As Khan explained, "Our model is to learn math the way you'd learn anything, like the way you would learn to ride a bicycle. Stay on that bicycle. Fall off that bicycle. Do it as long as necessary until you have mastery. The traditional model penalizes you for experimentation and failure, but it does not expect mastery. We encourage you to experiment. We encourage you to fail. But we do expect mastery."

What interests me so much about Khan's experience is that he was innovating teaching methods in an environment free of greedy bastards. His initial motivation was simply to help his cousins learn. His only priority was his students. He was in a position to offer his videos free of charge, so there was no money for a greedy bastard to try to skim. And he had no loyalty to the usual teaching technologies or the conventional teaching methods, because he wasn't a teacher at all. It's striking how quickly someone whose interests aligned with his students developed a radically different approach from the traditional classroom, and how much sense that approach makes for teaching a variety of subjects.

Find the Teachers Who Create Effective Learning Environments

Mike Milken's research on successful schools in the 1980s found that the "the number one factor was talent and ability of the teacher in the classroom," as he told me. This is borne out by the 1990s research of William Sanders, then a statistician at the University of Tennessee. As described in a report by Kati Haycock, president of the Education Trust, a nonpartisan DC think tank, Sanders ranked teachers in Tennessee based on how well their students performed. Then he divided a group of students who had performed at the same level and assigned some to the top-ranked teachers and some to the bottom-ranked teachers. "Students whose initial achievement levels are comparable have vastly different academic outcomes as a result of the sequence of teachers to which they are assigned," Haycock reported.

In another study, this one in Dallas, "the average reading scores of a group of fourth graders who were assigned to three highly effective teachers in a row rose from the 59th percentile in fourth grade to the 76th percentile by the conclusion of sixth grade. A fairly similar (but slightly higher-achieving) group of students was assigned three consecutive ineffective teachers and fell from the 60th percentile in fourth grade to the 42nd percentile by the end of sixth grade. A gap of this magnitude—more than 34 percentile points—for students who started off roughly the same is hugely significant."

Teachers are essential to creating effective learning environments, but the difficulty is finding the good ones and keeping them teaching. That's become more difficult, ironically, as an unintended consequence of feminism. Until the 1970s, when women were largely restricted in the number of professions they could choose, many of the smartest and best-educated young women went into teaching because it was one of the few intellectually challenging careers that would accept large numbers of women. Today many other professions benefit from greater numbers of women, but as Milken told me, "Many of our teachers, unfortunately, now come from the bottom of the class, not the top of the class."

We need roughly four million teachers in this country, and two other challenges make it hard to find good ones. First, there is what writer Malcolm Gladwell called the "quarterback problem" in an article for *The New Yorker*. Teaching, like playing quarterback, is a complex job requiring many different skills, and there is no simple way to test for the gift. As any football coach will tell you, you can't know who will make a good quarterback until you give that person a chance to get in the game. Similarly, there is no advance test for great teaching. You have to get in the classroom and try it. For that reason, we need a system that encourages many people to try teaching. That's what organizations such as Teach for America or Try Teaching do: attract large numbers of talented people—graduates of excellent colleges or professionals looking for a career change—to find out if they have what it takes.

Second, we need to hold on to the good teachers and let go of the ones who aren't as good. Traditionally, teachers have been rewarded and retained with security in the form of tenure and promotions based on seniority rather than results, but Louisiana is attempting to reverse that approach. As described in the *Washington Post*, the state keeps records on student achievement and evaluates teachers based on student success. Then the teachers are tracked back to their schools of education to discover which ones are producing the effective instructors. This motivates schools of education to update their approaches not according to someone's theory or some lawmaker's instruction but based, again, on what helps teachers foster environments where students actually learn. "It's accountability on steroids," said E. Joseph Savoie, president of the University of Louisiana at Lafayette.

Such an approach has implications for how—and how much—we pay teachers. If we are content to let teaching be a safe job that rewards seniority and draws from those who came from what Mike Milken called the bottom of the class, you won't have to pay teachers that much compared to other professionals. But if it's going to be a performance-based job you can lose if your students don't succeed and if we want people from the top of the class to take this job, then we're going to have to pay teachers better, aren't we?

The Louisiana model is one attempt to reverse the usual arrangement by recognizing that education is the train that carries us to learning. We must make students—traditionally the caboose on that train, pulled along behind administrators and teachers—into the engine. Whatever the results in Louisiana, one thing is certain: just by making the attempt, we will make a lot of greedy educational bastards unhappy.

To overcome their resistance, educational innovators will need the power to make changes. In Southern California, there is now a "parent trigger" law for public schools that gives parents new power to reform failing schools. As described on the website of Parent

Revolution, an education-reform group based in Los Angeles, if 51 percent of parents with children at a school feel that it is unable to function at an acceptable level, and if they sign an approved petition, then the parents win the legal right to force the school to remake itself by becoming a charter school, by turning over hiring and budgeting decisions to the local community, or by making less radical changes, such as hiring new administrators. Ben Austin, executive director of Parent Revolution, told me, "I'm not a medical doctor, but I know how to pick a pediatrician for my daughters, and I know whether they're getting good medical care or not. Same with schools. Parents don't need to know how to run a school" to judge whether it's time to hire a new staff with new priorities.

It remains to be seen how successful parents will be in reforming underperforming schools, but if nothing else, Parent Revolution has expressed the problem well. "Our schools," Austin said, "don't serve kids, because they're not designed to. They're designed to serve grown-ups. . . . The only way we're going to change things is to effectuate a radical and unapologetic transfer of raw power from the defenders of the status quo" to the parents. It's a matter of VICI values: parents are the ones whose interests are closest to those of the students, who need learning environments that prepare them for our fast-changing world.

But the danger that such a transfer of power presents from administrators to parents is that it offers frustrated families the satisfaction of tearing down what doesn't work without any guarantee that those who seize control can help students learn better. In chapter 4 on health care, Dr. Brenner suggested ways to redirect resources to create better health. How would we make comparable improvements in education?

The essential problem with education, like all of the industries we've seen in this book, is that our system is out of date. "We have a system of education that is modeled on the interests of industrialization and in the image of it," explained author and education expert Sir Kenneth Robinson in a speech for RSA Animate. "Schools are still pretty much organized on factory lines. Ringing bells, separate facilities specialized into separate subjects. We still educate children in batches. We put them through the system by age group. . . . It's like the most important thing about them is their date of manufacture."

Just as the point of the heath care system should be to improve health, not to sell procedures and drugs, so in a fast-changing world the emphasis in education should not be teaching or testing that is standardized on the model of last century's industry. And certainly not the prestige of expensive buildings and sports stadiums. We should reorganize education and redirect education funding to enable learning. And what has struck me as a journalist researching the best alternatives to the industrial factory model of schooling is how similar the answers are, all around the country. Whether I was walking through a STEM school in Seattle, visiting celebrated educator Nick Negroponte's lab in Cambridge, or touring the Khan Academy in San Francisco, I found the same basic values and goals for education reform:

1. Emphasize group-based problem solving. Most great learning, like most innovation in business, happens in groups. We need to help people learn the skills of cooperative innovation in school so they can use them for their entire lives

2. End age segregation. Students master different areas of study at different speeds and at different ages. Younger students learn by work-

ing with more experienced students, and older students learn by teaching younger students. Most work environments include people of different ages. For all these reasons, it will be more effective to stop restricting students to peers with the same "date of manufacture."

3. Encourage mistakes, but expect mastery. Encourage teachers to use hot-spotting within the classroom to identify areas where students need the most work. Then give them the time and the support to study those areas until they are mastered.

4. Emphasize and reward creative and divergent thought. In a time of rapid change, students must learn not just to find the answers that are waiting at the back of the book, but the answers—and the new questions—that no one expected when the book was written. As a nation, we need flexible thinkers who can keep learning and creating new approaches to problems as those problems evolve.

These should be the goals of every attempt to reform what Robinson calls the "habits and habitats" of our educational institutions, from kindergarten through college, so we can align the institutions with the best interests of the students and the changing needs of our society.

6

Breaking the Oil Pushers' Grip

What if one change could make us richer, more productive, safer from our enemies, and truer to our values of freedom and democracy? What if achieving this goal would create jobs and improve the environment for generations to come? What if Republican and Democratic presidents from Nixon through Obama had already endorsed it? Would you support such a change? One change.

I realize, it sounds like a fantasy. Does it require some specula-

tive technology that is decades or centuries away from practical use? In fact, no. The technology already exists. I'm talking about the technology to free our country from dependence on foreign oil. President Nixon said in 1974 that we needed to be energy independent by 1980. President Gerald Ford said it was vital to our national interests. President Jimmy Carter said that reliance on foreign oil was a clear and present danger to our nation. President George W. Bush acknowledged that "America is addicted to oil."

What do we do with all that expensive oil we buy? As with fuels in general, the main thing we do with it is this: we throw it away. Because oil is so essential to transportation, and because historically we have been leaders in industrial technology, you might assume that America would use fuel efficiently. Don't we have an efficiency standard for energy mandated by our president? Yes, but that president was Dwight Eisenhower, and the standard—which has not been raised since his administration in the 1950s—is 34 percent according to the US Department of Energy Information Administration. In other words, for every unit of fuel we burn to create energy in a stationary power facility, one-third serves us productively, and the other two-thirds disappear into the air as heat. In addition, according to Eric Isaacs, director of the US Department of Energy's Argonne National Laboratory, slightly more than a third of home energy loss (35 percent) occurs through air leaks. And in 2010 alone, disruptions in our antiquated and inefficient power grids cost our country over $100 billion.

It doesn't have to be this way. In Germany and Japan, where they use heat-capture technology to make productive use of the heat before it escapes, the efficiency ratio is 80 percent or better in power plants. The technology is not even that complex. Essentially, they place a shell over the power plant, capture the heat as it releases, and cycle it back to run the furnaces. And it's not new. Tom Casten is chairman of Recycled Energy Development, a company that helps manufacturers reduce energy costs through heat recycling. As Casten explained to me, when Thomas Edison built his first power generating plant in New York, he used the heat created by the exhaust to warm nearby buildings.

It's shocking how much fuel we waste in American power plants, but when it comes to oil for transportation, it's even worse. Let's say that you put ten gallons of gas in your conventional gas-powered car or SUV or truck. How much of that moves the car forward? As Bob Deans, associate director of communications for the environmental action group Natural Resources Defense Council, explained on my show, the first six gallons are wasted by the inefficiency of the engine and are lost to heat and friction. Two more gallons burn off when the car idles at stop signs and stoplights, or as it waits for passengers to get in or out. Only the last two gallons move the car where you want to go. We pay for ten and use two.

Our extreme energy inefficiency is not just expensive, it's dangerous. Most of our military enemies around the world profit from all the oil we buy. As Glenn Hurowitz of the Center for International Policy, a foreign-policy think tank blogged, "Osama bin Laden's rise was made possible by oil money. He acquired the millions of dollars that allowed him to start and finance al Qaeda from his huge family construction business, which literally paved the way for Saudi Arabia's massive oil boom." Hurowitz named the leaders whose brutal regimes were made possible by oil: Mu'ammar Gadhafi held out for months against a domestic rebellion and a NATO (North Atlantic Treaty Organization) air campaign with the oil money that paid mercenaries and bought off opponents. Iran's Mahmoud Ahmadinejad used oil money to finance the terrorist groups Hezbollah and Hamas, as well as his own multibillion-dollar nuclear weapons program. Bahrain's royal family hired Saudi troops to put down a democratic reform movement. And Russian prime minister Vladimir Putin can ignore calls for openness and economic innovation because of oil money.

Oil profits support our enemies and prop up dictators all around the world. As financier and natural gas advocate T. Boone Pickens calculated, if oil averages $100 a barrel for a year, countries belonging to the Organization of Petroleum Exporting Countries (OPEC) will make $1 trillion. A *trillion*. Not only might that money go to our enemies, but it's also not available for productive investment here at home, meaning lost opportunities for new businesses and new jobs. Half of our monthly trade extraction is due to rigged Chinese trade; the other half, to foreign oil, so our oil addiction weakens us both militarily and economically. Shifting to domestic energy sources is not just a matter of economics, it's a matter of patriotism. "In order for America to be safe," James Woolsey, former director of the CIA, told me, "we must shatter the strategic dependence on petroleum."

When Nixon first advocated energy independence, we imported 24 percent of our oil. Now it's 67 percent. "If we don't do anything," Pickens told me recently, "in ten years we'll import seventy-five percent of our oil, and you'll pay three hundred dollars a barrel for it." That's three times the price we pay today, and *one hundred times* the price we paid in the early 1970s.

How can the United States end its dangerous dependency? Centuries ago, many nations faced the same question about, of all things, salt. Before there were refrigerators, salt was the main way to preserve food, from dried meats to pickled vegetables. If you ruled a country and your country ran out of salt, your people wouldn't last the winter—and before they died, they'd come after you in violent rage. Nations went to war over salt mines. The Roman Empire used salt for money, which in time gave us the word "salary." The expression "You are salt of the earth" meant that you represented what was best and most noble in society.

Then refrigeration was invented. As Woolsey put it at the energy summit that I convened at Oklahoma State University in 2011, "Refrigeration destroyed salt's strategic role. We still use it, still put it on the sidewalks in winter, and eat in on corn on the cob. But nobody looks at the salt shaker when they go to the table and wonders if we're salt independent." With the adoption of new food-preservation technologies, salt became boring. That must be our goal in the fight for energy independence: we must adopt the innovative technologies that will make oil boring.

But it's one thing to tell an addict to give up his habit and try a better way of life; it's another to get him do it. For forty years, American presidents have been saying that we need to end our oil dependence, yet we're not much closer than when President Nixon stated the goal. What keeps us hooked? To understand how America got addicted to oil, and how it prevents us from taking steps that almost everyone agrees would strengthen the country, we have to reboard my time machine and travel back to the days of whaling ships—and the rise of the greedy bastards who profit by keeping us dependent on petroleum, even today.

The No-Longer-Free Market for Oil

Oil in America used to come mainly from whales. Fishermen would catch whales in the Atlantic Ocean and bring them to ports in New England and New York, where the blubber was refined into oil and carried in railroad cars to light city streetlamps, among other things. But as petroleum deposits were discovered in the United States and refining costs fell, this resource became cheaper than whale oil. Whaling died out, as outmoded industries are supposed to do.

The early market for petroleum was volatile and competitive. Supply fluctuated, and price with it—that's how supply and demand are supposed to work in a free market. But greedy bastards prefer the opposite: ideally, a rigged market with reliably manipulated pricing.

The first of the modern greedy bastards, an owner of an oil refining company, John D. Rockefeller, had the idea that he could stabilize prices by controlling supply—that is, limit oil available to customers as a way to drive the price high and keep it there. In 1870 he founded the Standard Oil Company and began using its profits to buy up competitors.

As Les Manns, a professor of economics at Doane College in Crete, Nebraska, explains, some of Rockefeller's competitors were content to sell their refining operations to him. When they weren't, he and his partners used a set of tactics not widely known then. They relied on industrial espionage—spying—to learn a competitor's financial situation, and then lowered their oil price near or below the competitor's cost, making it difficult, if not impossible, for the competitor to stay in business.

Standard Oil soon grew large enough that it could use this tactic without suffering any loss of its own; it lowered prices in the competitor's region while raising them elsewhere in the country to make up the difference in income. In this way, the company charged its customers a premium to drive the competition out of business, which then left those same customers even more dependent on Standard Oil. Rockefeller referred to this approach as "sweating" the competition. Even just the threat was enough to induce some competitors to sell, because a potential rival that had been nearly bankrupted by Rockefeller's sweating would sell for less than a rival that simply accepted an earlier offer. By 1882, Standard Oil controlled 80 percent to 90 percent of the oil refining capacity in the United States.

Rockefeller applied further pressure to his competition by making special deals with the railroads that carried his oil. Lake Shore Railroad, part of New York Central, granted Rockefeller a 70 percent discount for committing to transport large quantities of oil every day—quantities too big for any competitor to match. Standard Oil's influence over the railroads was so great that it could effectively prevent competitors from shipping their product at all. In one famous case, a competitor that was denied rail transport tried to build a pipeline to carry its oil. Rockefeller stopped the company by directing the railroad to refuse permission for the pipeline to cross its land.

By 1899, Standard controlled retail, wholesale, oil fields, and refining. Prices had been "stabilized" at a level far higher than market rates. Rockefeller had neutralized the power of the free market for his own personal benefit, and he was well on his way to becoming the country's first billionaire—and, in inflation-adjusted terms, the richest man in history.

Then in 1902 the writer Ida Tarbell, daughter of a man whose company had been sweated out of business, began a series of nineteen articles for *McClure's Magazine* explaining the ways of the greedy bastards at Standard Oil. Collected into a book that the *New York Times* later ranked as one of the twentieth century's top five works of investigative journalism, her exposé sparked nationwide anger and helped lead to the antitrust proceedings that in 1911 broke Standard Oil into thirty-four regional companies. The company's reputation was so damaged that it stopped using the name Standard Oil, leading to many of the familiar oil company names we know today: Standard Oil of New Jersey eventually became Exxon, Standard Oil of New York became Mobil, and so forth.

But while the courts that broke up Standard Oil took Tarbell's testimony on the business practices that created the Standard Oil monopoly, either they didn't understand Rockefeller's greedy-bastard tactics or they chose not to block them. Former Standard Oil stockholders received an equal percentage of stock in the new subsidiaries as they'd held in the original company. Within a year after the court broke up Rockefeller's behemoth, the collective stock price of the "new" companies had risen over 100 percent. Later, from the 1940s to the early 1970s, several remerged Standard Oil companies, working in concert with Royal Dutch Shell and British Petroleum and known together as the Seven Sisters, controlled not just America's oil reserves but also the world's. In 1973, for example, the seven companies claimed 85 percent of the planet's oil supply.

But in the 1970s, America's demand for oil grew beyond domestic supply for the first time. As the US economy became dependent on imported oil, power shifted to OPEC, the organization of oil-exporting countries mainly in the Middle East and Africa.

OPEC's founding statute described its purpose as "stabilization of prices in international oil markets with a view to eliminating harmful and unnecessary fluctuations [due to the] necessity of securing a steady income." OPEC, in other words, is a cartel modeled after Rockefeller's Standard Oil, with the power to keep prices high by limiting the flow of oil. OPEC did just that in 1973, cutting supply and raising the price of crude oil from $3 a barrel to $12 a barrel. Many analysts cite this move as the cause of the stock market slump of 1973–74 and the subsequent recession.

But even after control of oil reserves shifted overseas, refining remained in the hands of the former Standard Oil companies. And they have continued Rockefeller's tactic of limiting refining capacity to keep gas prices artificially high. As described in the 2011 documentary *Gashole*, codirected by Jeremy Wagener and Scott D. Roberts, American oil companies have actually reduced refining capacity in the last fifteen years, so that only a one- or two-week supply is available. When national disasters such as 9/11 or Hurricane Katrina disrupt refining or distribution networks to even a small degree, the threat to supply provokes a panic in the markets, turning the national disaster into an opportunity for extra oil company profits. For example, in the course of Hurricane Katrina in 2005, major product distribution pipelines in the Gulf of Mexico were hit. The price of gasoline futures shot up immediately, according to Richard Karp of the American Petroleum Institute, the major trade association of the US oil and natural gas industry, and consumers were shocked to see gasoline prices tick up to $5.50 and $6 per gallon. This greedy-bastard tactic has persisted despite multiple congressional investigations.

These disasters bring up the specter of the 2011 disaster at

Japan's Fukushima Daiichi nuclear power plant and the British Petroleum oil spill in the Gulf of Mexico the year before. In both cases, we discovered too late that safety systems were being ignored. Both companies were using their host government as unpaid insurance companies, left to pay the bills and clean up the damage when the energy industry's risky bets go wrong. While the history of oil in America involves various twists and turns—the discovery of reserves in Alaska and the Gulf, the oil glut of the 1980s—the underlying constant is clear. Almost since oil became the basis for transportation, the United States has been dependent on an oil industry controlled by an evolving series of similar monopolies with government blessing. At first it was domestic and now it is foreign, but the ability to influence and often control the no-longer-free market for energy has remained historically consistent.

Breaking the Grip

Rockefeller's tactics got America hooked on oil, but what keeps us from kicking the habit? In theory, all it would take is to find ways to use oil more efficiently or to create fuels not made from petroleum. And though that may sound like science fiction, there have been workable alternatives to oil from the beginning of the automobile age. As far back as the 1890s, Rudolf Diesel invented the diesel engine. It is more efficient than the gasoline-powered engine because its temperature rises more slowly; consequently, more energy goes into movement and less is wasted as heat. But Diesel was not just an inventor of another way to burn oil. A social visionary and writer, he hoped that his engine would allow craftsmen and artisans to compete more effectively with big industry. His engine ran as well on peanut oil as it did on petroleum-based fuel, and he hoped to run engines on other innovative fuels such as coal dust.

Diesel might have led an early-twentieth-century movement away from strict reliance on oil and toward a world in which cars ran on many different fuels, but one night on a boat to London, he went to his cabin to sleep and disappeared. Ten days later, his drowned body was recovered from the ocean. The circumstances of his death have never been explained, but although his diesel engine is used around the world, it is used exclusively with petroleum-based fuel. The opportunity that Diesel and his engine might lead a movement toward energy alternatives was lost for more than a century.

After Rudolf Diesel, the history of attempts to move beyond oil in the twentieth century becomes a nonhistory. In our astonishingly inventive country, every road that might have led toward greater efficiency or more alternatives turned out to be a dead end. Jeremy Wagener and Scott D. Roberts document many of these mysteriously disappointing innovations: the 1946 Buick Roadmaster that got one hundred miles per gallon; the fuel-efficiency patents that were bought up by car companies and supposedly buried; the secret research into the possibility of an engine that got a thousand miles per gallon; and the engine modifications carried out in the 1970s by a mechanic named Tom Ogle. The young Texan's innovation, which vaporized fuel to get one hundred miles per gallon, was never used commercially after his apparent suicide. All these stories end one of two ways: either the oil companies buy up the rights to these inventions and bury them or the inventor himself is buried.

Were these stories true? I don't know. And with so much constructive work to be done, we don't have time to vet old conspiracy theories. But every time I hear another tale of the lost breakthroughs of the past century, it strikes me how often what they describe is the same greedy-bastard techniques that Ida Tarbell first revealed in her groundbreaking work on Standard Oil.

The Death and Rebirth of the Electric Car

The closest we came to an alternative to the gas-powered car was the electric car. As described in Chris Paine's 2006 documentary *Who Killed the Electric Car?*, electric vehicles were popular at the beginning of the twentieth century. They were quiet, they produced no pollution, and you didn't have to crank the engine. But once the gas car became dominant, no electric car was marketed for almost a century.

Then in 1987 General Motors got some welcome publicity when its team of innovators won the world solar race with an experimental electric car. Chairman Roger Smith started an initiative for the company to build an electric car for sale to the public. It sounded like a win-win venture: General Motors would get a new product to sell, the EV1, not to mention the public relations value of being a successful innovator with its eyes on the future. Consumers would get a quiet, clean vehicle that needed no engine tune-ups and could get a gallon's worth of driving from sixty cents' worth of electricity. They could plug it into a wall outlet at home to recharge.

As the new cars became available for lease, the California Air Resources Board (CARB), a state regulatory agency, became interested in the EV1. The board was looking for solutions to the ongoing health crisis from smog: at that time, one out of four young people in Los Angeles County suffered from severe lung lesions and chronic respiratory disease. Inspired by the EV1, in 1990 the board passed the Zero Emissions Mandate. The mandate would mean that any company selling cars in California would have at least 2 percent of their vehicles be zero-emissions cars by 1998. The minimum would then rise to 5 percent in 2001 and 10 percent in 2003.

GM offered the EV1 through its Saturn dealerships and launched the car with a memorable Super Bowl advertisement that showed toasters, blenders, and other electric household appliances walking out of their suburban homes to meet the EV1 in the driveway. Waiting lists for the new vehicles began to grow. Not wanting to be left behind, Toyota, Honda, Ford, Nissan, and Chrysler all began manufacturing electric cars. For the first time in nearly a century, there were nonpolluting, moderately priced, domestically sourced alternatives to gasoline-powered cars. What had been a mere concept and a PR coup for GM had become a practical alternative to feeding the greedy bastards in oil. How did this happen? Through a fortunate convergence of free-market competition and VICI values.

Then the Western States Petroleum Association, a lobbying group for the oil industry, began working in secret to oppose the Zero Emissions Mandate, which had required greater transparency and integrity regarding the hidden costs of gas-powered transportation. The association funded fake consumer groups with fraudulent lists of sponsors to protest CARB's efforts to build public car-charging stations, damaging the integrity of the political process.

GM itself began petitioning CARB to reverse the Zero Emissions Mandate, arguing that there was no consumer demand for the electric car. The car company launched a new ad campaign, supposedly intended to market the EV1, which showed the car in blighted landscapes suggesting the end of civilization. Potential customers, even well-known movie stars, were required to provide extensive personal information as part of an increasingly difficult "application" for the privilege of leasing an electric car. GM employees even began calling potential customers on its waiting lists to "inform" them of the potential drawbacks of the EV1. In all these ways, the movie suggests, GM deliberately worked to reduce visibility and intentionally confuse consumers about the choice of an electric car, in order to sabotage its prospects.

In 2002, the Bush administration joined a lawsuit against California's mandate. Around the same time, the White House announced a $1.2 billion grant to develop hydrogen fuel cells in cars. Governor Arnold Schwarzenegger of California toured the state in a hydrogen-powered Hummer to raise awareness of the potential of hydrogen fuel cells, but no hydrogen-fueled cars were ever offered to the public because hydrogen technology was still at an early, exploratory stage. (The cost for the infrastructure to make hydrogen cars practical across the country would top $400 million, according to hydrogen energy expert Dr. Venki Raman.) A speculative, hypothetical alternative fuel was being offered in place of a proven technology already on the roads.

Finally, Dr. Alan Lloyd, the chair of CARB, who had defended the Zero Emissions Mandate for twelve years, accepted an additional post as the director of the new California Fuel Cell Partnership—a new prohydrogen organization! He then agreed to reverse most of CARB's zero emissions mandate.

What happened to the cars themselves? Almost five thousand electric cars had been manufactured for leasing to California, including the EV1, the Toyota RAV4 EV, and the Honda EV Plus.

Energy

Every choice to align the interests of energy users and efficiency reduces our military entanglements, cuts our trade deficit, increases our freedom, and preserves our planet; every choice to breach it destroys it.

Where does the money go?

War
Military engagements are paid for by US taxpayers to secure passage to privately owned oil reserves.

Environment
Environmental harm, sometimes massive, is paid for by the people and the planet, with a minimal proportional fee paid by private industry.

Short-Term Results
• Relatively cheap gas
• US-financed global military conflict in energy-rich regions
• The occasional mega-disaster (BP, Fukushima)
• Reverse hot-spotting effect as money pours into fossil fuels, depriving investment for clean replacements
• Imported oil accounts for one half of the US trade deficit = lost jobs

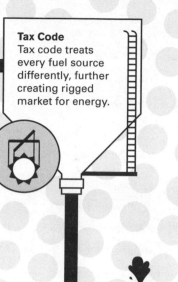

Tax Code
Tax code treats every fuel source differently, further creating rigged market for energy.

Long-Term Results
• National dependence on an increasingly expensive, dirty, and dangerous fuel source
• Failure to adapt to more efficient cars, homes, and factories
• Failure to develop alternative fuels and fuel delivery systems
• Risk to national independence

Government
Our bought government refuses to be honest about the real costs of energy and refuses to alter the tax code to reward upgrades to efficient households, factories, and transportation.

THE FIX

1 For breach 1 and 2 begin a 5 percent a year gas tax to more closely represent the real cost being incurred for oil. Pay all tax proceeds in full equally as a dividend back to all Americans—by doing this the market rewards efficiency and punishes waste.

2 Create a flat tax and subsidy law to force all fuel sources to be treated equally by the government.

3/4 Tell your politicians you know how much our dependence on foreign oil is harming the USA. Demand update of Eisenhower-era efficiency standards into the twenty-first century.

When drivers tried to renew their leases, the requests were denied. Owners who did not return their cars to the dealerships were threatened with legal action. A group of activists pledged nearly $2 million to buy eighty-two remaining EV1s, but its offer was refused. Nearly all of the vehicles were recalled and crushed. The new consumer choice was gone. VICI values had been defeated by vampire values.

In this story, you can see the techniques by which the unholy alliance of business and state keeps vampire industries in power: pressuring, enticing, and bribing politicians to change the rules to benefit the vampire industry, using force to overcome free-market competition, and the media sideshow that amuses and distracts—in this case, the photogenic Governor Schwarzenegger stepping out of an impractical, unripe new technology, the hydrogen Hummer.

What did American automakers do after engineering the death of the electric car? They again used their influence in government, which again rewrote the rules to afford them easier and more oil-industry-friendly ways to make money. As described in *High and Mighty: SUVs—The World's Most Dangerous Vehicles and How They Got That Way* by Keith Bradsher, American Motors Corporation lobbied the US Environmental Protection Agency (EPA) for a waiver of the Clean Air Act of 1963, to allow it to market sport-utility vehicles as "light trucks." This would exempt AMC from fuel efficiency requirements. The favor from the federal government made selling inefficient, polluting SUVs dramatically more profitable than efficient, greener cars. As Bradsher notes, for example, each sale of an Excursion SUV earned Ford a profit of $18,000, while the Ford Focus, a compact car that met federal fuel-efficiency guidelines, earned no profit at all unless the buyer bought optional features.

All of the Big Three automakers now funnel their ingenuity and their marketing dollars into selling these profitable, polluting gas-guzzlers.

GM Joins the Banksters

At the time, the financial services industry was making enormous profits by borrowing money at the historically low interest rates maintained by the Fed's Alan Greenspan, and then lending that money to the credit casino again. General Motors realized that in letting banks control the financing of car loans, it was missing out on an enormous opportunity: to borrow money cheaply for thirty days at a time and then loan it to car purchasers at an interest rate of 5 percent to 10 percent. GM founded General Motors Auto Credit (GMAC). Every month, it would borrow the money again. It was like being paid to let your entire life run on credit cards. Thanks to the federal loophole that made SUVs wildly profitable and the low government interest rates that turned General Motors into a financial institution, the company was free to ignore the waste and environmental damage of the low-efficiency vehicles it sold. In a sense, it wasn't GM's problem anymore: General Motors was no longer primarily a car company but was now in the light truck and banking businesses, too. It sold fuel-efficient cars as a way to bring up the "fleet average" for miles per gallon. This approach was highly profitable until the financial crisis of 2008, when the thirty-day credit markets closed up. And when the bailouts came, GM was bailed out too, not just because its 263,000 employees and numerous suppliers were at risk, but because it was essentially a bank, and the banks were "too big to fail."

The Real Price of Gas

Have I been unfair to General Motors? The carmaker's explanation for terminating the EV1 program has been that the decision was a simple response to market realities. Consumers were not interested enough in a nongasoline car to make it profitable, the company claimed. One issue was the range of a battery-powered car, which at first was only a hundred miles per charge. But 90 percent of car drivers use their cars for short commutes, for which a limited-range car would be ideal. The other was the price of gas. Why spend extra for a fuel-efficient car when gas is still cheap compared to places such as Europe or Japan, where the price of gas has tended to be three or four times higher than here?

I can understand drivers choosing to stick with the gasoline-powered cars and the cheap gas that they have, but that decision doesn't allow the free market to work. The price of gas is a false price. The real price of gasoline should be far higher than it is at the pump. But how can it be true that the price of oil is so high, as I've already said, and at the same time that it should be far higher?

The price of anything you buy has two components: what it costs to make plus the markup that the seller adds to make a profit. I've already described how since the days of Rockefeller and Standard Oil, oil companies have limited US refining in order to artificially lower supply and raise price. And they still do it today. They manipulate supply to justify increasing their markups. They charge more even though they haven't had to pay more to produce it. And they keep those manipulated profits, which is why oil companies frequently top the list of the most profitable corporations in the world.

But when it comes to the other component of price—how

much it costs oil companies to supply American demand for oil—
the industry has used its influence to strong-arm politicians into
giving it the same kind of outrageous, half-communist deal as the
banksters. When banks make profits, as we saw, they get to keep
them, but when they face big losses, the government (taxpayers like
you and me) covers their costs. Same for the oil industry. At the
pump, the price is between $3 and $4 a gallon. But that doesn't factor in the following:

- The costs for our military presence in oil-producing areas: aircraft
  carriers, foreign bases, troop deployment, and so forth. The military
  spends about $15 billion each year just on fuel, US Secretary of the
  Army John McHugh told United Press International.
- The medical and environmental costs of pollution from dirty energy
  sources. Not just the dramatic disasters but also the quieter harm
  such as the medical costs and the personal impact on the children
  of Los Angeles County who grow up with lesions on their lungs from
  smog.
- The costs of government subsidies for oil companies hidden in our
  tax code, which, according to Bob Deans of the National Resources
  Defense Council, the White House's Office of Management and Budget estimates officially at $46 billion over the next ten years. However,
  former CIA director James Woolsey said they might be five times that
  much, explaining, "You get a lot of disagreement about how much
  they are total. There are a lot of subsidies for oil that have been in the
  tax code for a long time. . . . It depends on what you count."

When you include these off-balance-sheet costs, the real price
of gas by my calculation is between $10 and $15 a gallon. Michael

Milken and his economic think tank the Milken Institute pegged it at $14 per gallon. But that number, several times the price we pay at the pump, can't reflect the human cost of our energy policies. Ashwin Madia, an attorney and veteran of the Iraq War, put it this way at my energy summit: "Think about just the past ten years, and how many young men and women we've sent overseas to be deployed in these countries. How many kids have lost their arms because of our dependence on oil or how many kids have lost their legs because of our dependence on oil? How many kids have suffered mental illness and so forth? How many families have been affected when their sons or daughters come home like this or maybe even don't come home at all? Those too are costs of our addiction to oil."

I'm not going to try to put a price tag on the human losses we suffer in protecting the flow of foreign oil. I'll leave that to you. For now, let's just stick with the straight economics. The price of gas at the pump is $3 to $4, but the real cost is $10 to $15. Who makes up the difference? The American taxpayer. It comes out of your taxes and mine. Are you satisfied with that?

In some ways, all we have to do to ratchet up demand for clean energy is to get rid of these off-balance-sheet costs of oil. We saw what even the doubling of gas prices could do in 2008, when gas hit $4 a gallon. Why was the price higher? In part because OPEC, like Standard Oil before it, was reaching the limit of its ability to feed the world's demand, with China and India consuming increasing amounts of oil. At the same time, as we saw in chapter 2 on finance, the crisis in the financial markets drove enormous amounts of money into commodities for safekeeping. That meant investors were bidding up the price of oil. In response to higher gas prices, demand for SUVs and pickup trucks collapsed. In June 2008, CNNMoney reported that GM, facing ongoing losses in North America, had announced closings of factories making SUVs and trucks, and approved production of the Volt, a plug-in hybrid car with both a battery and a gasoline engine. What was breaking the grip of the greedy bastards? The biggest piece was a moderately higher price for gas. At the new price, GM couldn't make a profit selling gas-guzzlers—not even with special favors from politicians. Chris Isidore of CNNMoney observed, "The plant-closing plans are a stunning admission from the nation's largest automaker that its long dependence on large SUVs and pickups is no longer a viable strategy."

Chris Paine, who wrote and directed *Who Killed the Electric Car?*, described two other factors when he came on my show in 2011 to discuss the sequel, *Revenge of the Electric Car*. The first was consumer pressure. Growing consumer awareness of green alternatives had turned GM's decision to kill the electric car into a lasting public relations problem. In the second film, Paine interviews one GM executive who wonders aloud what he has to do to convince customers that GM is "not Darth Vader." Paine also quotes Carlos Ghosn, CEO of Nissan, another car company facing serious losses. Ghosn bet the future of his company on the decision to spend $6 billion developing the fully electric Nissan Leaf and marketing it worldwide. "It's not an issue if global warming is right or wrong," he says, "but that the public expects this, and it will change the face of the brand and the industry."

The other factor Paine described was a weakening, if not yet a real break, in the unholy alliance between government and the oil and car companies. Although the Obama administration has not ended subsidies for the oil industry or reduced the impact of energy industry lobbyists, it has shown a willingness to "pressure the energy industries," as Paine put it, and to support green innovation. When Tesla Motors ran into serious financial difficulties developing electric cars, the Department of Energy provided a loan that reassured investors and sustained the company until its initial public offering of stock restored its operating budget. The company, which had been on the brink of bankruptcy, went on to show a profit beginning in July 2009. Without that support, Tesla vehicles might have gone the way of the EV1. Federal tax credits of $7500 have also been helpful.

The result of these changes has been a shift to a broad wave of innovations, not only from GM, Nissan, Tesla, and Toyota but also from hundreds of small innovators who convert existing cars to run on batteries. As *New York Times* columnist Thomas Friedman states in the documentary, "This is real-scale industrial innovation and deployment." Paine believes that there is a window of opportunity to end the dominance of transportation by gas-powered vehicles that will last as long as there is a Democratic administration. In that period, if consumers buy electric cars, it will "show companies it can work." This would be the *beginning* of a solution: remember, even if every car were electric, we would still need to update our wasteful electric power grid.

But breaking the grip of the greedy bastards and returning the auto industry to open competition in a free market will be much easier than doing the same with the oil companies, which are far larger. As Bob Deans told me, oil is "the wealthiest, most profitable industry in the history of the world. It has made one trillion dollars in profits over just the last decade, and it has an army in Washington of nearly eight hundred lobbyists who wake up every morning and say, 'Whose palm can I grease? Whose arm can I twist to make sure that my shareholders' profits are well represented in our energy policy?'"

Still, in the end, even the greediest of greedy-bastard decisions are business decisions. In GM's case, the company got back into the efficient-car business when price integrity in our fuel costs changed customer behavior. Suddenly the carmakers, customers, and the planet have found aligned interests and adapted.

In the same way, if we can shatter our country's strategic dependence on petroleum, then the executives at Exxon Mobil, Chevron, and the others will find it in their economic interests to become long-term greedy. We know that is possible because it was true in the past: oil companies, along with the auto industry, were the prime lobbyists behind the interstate highway system of 1956, the largest public works project of all time. It increased demand for oil and cars, so it was profitable to both industries, but at the same time, it built new national infrastructure, created jobs, and gave Americans the mobility to go where the jobs were.

This Generation's Mission to the Moon

There is a silver bullet that will kill the vampire of the incumbent energy industry: efficiency. We are lost in a debate over which fuel is best when what we need to talk about is getting more from every fuel we use. So what is the best fuel for America or the world going forward? Efficiency. In fact, increasing efficiency offers the immediate possibility to defund our enemies, halve our trade deficit, create millions of jobs, end the wars, improve the environment, and realign international interests.

Our power generation is only 34 percent efficient, but it doesn't have to be that way. In Germany today, the government doesn't hide the extra costs of energy as secret taxes and budget tricks, they tax gasoline where everyone can see it and use the money to fund heat-capture technology to boost efficiency and alternative fuels to end the country's reliance on oil. We need to stop rewarding our utilities for inefficiency and protecting them from competition. What they need is not corporate communism but practical incentives, with aligned interests to become more efficient.

But the shift to efficiency is not just a matter of change at the national level. We need change at every level: at the state and local levels, and among families and individuals as well. As individuals, we need to bring back one of the greatest warriors in the fight for efficiency and against terrorism: your nagging grandmother. The one who tells you to close the refrigerator until you decide what you want to eat. Turn off the lights when you leave a room. Get that car in for a tune-up and make sure they check the pressure in the tires. The problem is, sometimes you do it, and sometimes you don't. But what if you had to pay real costs for expensive decisions?

Think about what a national plan to restore price integrity would do at the kitchen table. If we knew that every car, house, and power plant in America was required to make an annual 5 percent increase in efficiency, it would make energy efficiency part of the dinner table conversation.

At the consumer level, we can support this movement toward greater efficiency by building requirements for efficiency into every major transaction. When you buy a house or a car, there could be a tax incentive to help everybody upgrade to more efficient technologies. The same approach could be used with permits to run power plants.

Where efficiency has been tried, it has succeeded wildly.

- California has achieved consistent energy efficiency gains for three decades, and the cost of power per kilowatt of "efficiency" is about one-fifth that of generating a kilowatt from coal, nuclear power, or natural gas.

- Dow Chemical's Louisiana division held a contest to identify and fund energy-saving projects from 1982 to 1993, and the return on investment ranged between 170 percent and 340 percent a year.

- Opower, a software company that partners with utility companies to increase energy efficiency, has saved 215 million kilowatts of electricity by working with utilities to encourage customers to turn off the lights.

Germany has a plan to be off oil and nuclear power by 2050 by emphasizing efficiency and alternative technologies such as wind and solar. We have no plan at all. Many of us think of China as a country oppressed and behind the times, but it has better energy efficiency technology than we do. We need to recognize that America has fallen behind in a race it might well lose. When it comes to clean energy overall, the United States was the world leader until 2008, but according to the Pew Environment Group, we have been pushed to third by China, which "attracted a record $54.4 billion in clean energy investments in 2010—a 39 percent increase over 2009.... Germany saw private investments double to $41.2 billion and was second in the G-20, up from third last year." Michael Liebreich, CEO of Bloomberg New Energy Finance, explained, "The US has not been creating demand for deployment of clean energy. As a result, it is losing out on opportunities to attract investment, create manufacturing capabilities, and spur job growth. For example, worldwide, China is now the leading manufacturer of wind turbines and solar panels."

We are falling behind, but, then, we fell behind the old Soviet Union once as well. In 1957 the Russians launched the Sputnik satellite into orbit, and we looked up at the sky and worried. And then we took action. The tools existed then, and we had the will to use them. The tools for achieving energy independence exist today.

In March 2011, President Obama set a goal that in ten years we will import a third less oil than we do today. I think we deserve a president who will promote a much more daring policy than that. Back in 1961, faced with a Soviet Union bent on dominating the world and well ahead of us in the manned space race, President John F. Kennedy embarked us on a mission to the Moon. At the time, it seemed foolish to think that we could land a man on the Moon by the end of the decade. Yet we did it.

What exactly should we do today? We should support the newer technologies (as we have supported oil and nuclear for decades) until they are ready to compete in the free market. As the Pew research shows, the nations that attract the most clean energy investment are the ones with national plans in place. We have no plan, which means that our default plan is foreign oil—more and more of it, at an ever-increasing price.

As increased price integrity allows clean energy alternatives to stand on their own two feet, then the best alternatives can win. I don't know which will prove best, and neither do you—that's why I'm so interested in fostering innovation and competition. What I do know is that individually and as a country we need to rethink transportation and power generation everywhere we look. We need to look at the energy grid in terms of what can provide the most efficient energy for each type of asset. Maybe buildings should be geothermal, because they're already low to the ground and can make use of that energy for heating and cooling. Maybe bus stops in the middle of nowhere should have their lights and heat powered by solar panels, because they are expensive to hook up to the power grid. Picture a global quilt of variable energy sources, with annual incentives to burn less fuel and find more sources from "above the earth," as John Hofmeister, former president of the Shell Oil Company, puts it. Now imagine that this global quilt provides electricity to the two billion people who currently rely for fuel on burning wood and cow dung—just think how the world changes.

Until I convened my energy summit, I didn't understand either how dangerous our current energy practices are—or how eminently solvable our energy problem is. Once I saw how much we have to lose or gain with energy sourcing, it became apparent how important VICI values are. A single breach of price integrity—the hidden price of gas—has left us with a multitrillion dollar, multidecade cascade of unnecessary expenditure, global pollution, and conflict. But just as health care can be far more efficient, so energy can far more efficient as well. Now it's a question of politics and some very creative thinking: how do we build our communities so that people can live the way they want while conserving energy? How can we responsibly balance the promise of a domestic fuel like natural gas against the environmental damage that can be caused by taking it out of the ground? How best to arrange fast rail service so that people who don't want to own cars have that choice? No one has the answers to all of these questions, but we do know how to get answers: coordinated American ingenuity and open competition toward a shared goal, with shared problem-solving values.

The Unholy Alliance

A US senator once asked me, "Does the government regulate Wall Street, or does Wall Street, with their billions and billions of dollars, regulate the government through lobbying and campaign financing?" He was talking about the finance industry, but he could have been describing any one of the vampire industries that uses its wealth and power to influence politicians.

Consider General Electric, the biggest corporation in America. In 2010, according to the *New York Times*, GE reported profits of $14.2 billion, of which $5.1 billion came from operations in the United States. What did the company pay in taxes that year? Nothing. Its tax bill was zero. And it gets worse: not only did GE pay nothing, but it collected tax benefits of $3.2 billion.

How? General Electric hired a team of former government officials, as the *Times* explained, "not just from the Treasury, but also from the IRS and virtually all the tax-writing committees in Congress." The company paid its now-private team of government officials to lobby for changes in the tax law that would benefit GE, and then it used a team of accountants and lawyers to exploit the loopholes it had lobbied to create. GE may be the best at this game, but many other corporations have learned how to influence tax law for their own benefit. Back in the 1950s, corporate taxes contributed 30 percent of the federal government's revenue. Today that number has fallen to less than 7 percent.

That's how corporate tax law works these days. It's a far cry from what most of us learned as kids about how laws are made. Remember "I'm Just a Bill," the *Schoolhouse Rock* song and cartoon that since 1975 has introduced generations of young Americans to the legislative process? It makes lawmaking sound very different. "When I started," the cartoon bill explains in between choruses, "I wasn't even a bill, I was just an idea. Some folks back home decided they wanted a law passed, so they called their local congressman, and he said, 'You're right, there oughta be a law.' Then he sat down and wrote me out and introduced me to Congress."

In its barest outline, this is correct. If the American people voice a concern consistently and loudly, their elected representatives will likely respond. When there was a loud, sustained outcry about our health care system—it's too expensive and excludes too many Americans—politicians heard the public's voice, and a version of a health care reform bill ultimately passed.

Public opinion for political change carries the day only if the people can remain focused. As each fresh news item grabs our attention, and as each groundswell of response is replaced by the next, public attention keeps shifting. In contrast to the distractible public, organized interests pay professional lobbyists to maintain focus and pressure patiently and relentlessly. According to the Center for Responsive Politics, a nonprofit group in Washington, DC, that tracks influence peddling in government, there are twenty-eight officially registered lobbyists in Washington for every single member of Congress. That's twenty-eight well-funded professionals paid to stay on message—that is, the message of the companies that hire them. In the health care reform debate, according to Bloomberg news, 3,300 lobbyists registered to work on the issue. In the first six months of 2009, health care companies spent $263 million on direct lobbying. Pharmaceutical companies alone spent $134 million. And health care is only one of many industries that use these tactics to influence the government to prevent change—spending money to protect their business model, not to make legislation better.

Bear in mind, few things are more democratic than advocating a policy idea. Even the authors of our constitution realized that citizens or groups of them, regardless of economic standing, must have the right to address their government and be heard. Lobbying is an essential service. But because of the unholy alliance, lobbyists wield influence based on their ability to raise money for or against a given policy, not based on the good of that policy.

For this reason it is critical to distinguish between our democratic right to address our government and money's toxic effect on that process. In other words, we need lobbyists, but we cannot have lobbyist-fund-raisers. I doubt our founding fathers, who invented "lobbying," ever intended to create fund-raisers masquerading as policy advocates. The constitution does not say you have the right to pay for access to your government. It says you have the right to address your government.

First, the Public Expresses Its Wishes

Let's follow the steps from public concern to signed law. To begin, of course, the public doesn't speak with one voice. We all need to make up our minds, issue by issue, before we decide that we want a law passed and what that law should be. There is a complex and ongoing political conversation that shapes ideas about what the problem is and how best to solve it.

In this conversation, we all rely on the media to frame the topic and help us decide which subjects are important. But the media, like all of the other industries I discuss in this book, has gone through a period of tremendous change. It used to be that the major media had "gatekeeper" power: if you were a politician and you wanted broad national exposure, you needed one of the major networks or one of a handful of major newspapers to interview you, and you had to face tough questions from the likes of *60 Minutes*'s Mike Wallace. But the Internet and talk radio have fragmented the media, creating many more outlets, so that politicians and other sources in the political discussion can afford to pick the outlets that will toss them softball questions.

For example, in my career as a financial reporter, I interviewed every secretary of the Treasury. During the last two years of the Bush administration, I used to host an economic summit at the White House with Hank Paulson and the economic cabinet. But in 2009, when I began asking tough political questions about the financial bailout, Paulson's successor as Treasury secretary, Tim Geithner, wouldn't agree to an interview with me. And he continues to refuse. He can do that because in the fragmented media landscape, with so many networks and so many Internet-based alternatives to networks, he has plenty of other places to give interviews. I can understand his choice—if I were Geithner, I wouldn't want to answer my tough questions, either!—but it's much easier today for him to avoid the hardball questions and still get his message out unchallenged to a wider audience than it would have been ten or twenty years ago.

The fragmented media world benefits more than just those who want to sidestep probing questions; it shifts the entire incentive for media away from solid reporting and toward stirring up public interest regardless of how truly newsworthy a story might be. Just look at how the murder trial of Florida mom Casey Anthony and the pricey nuptials of reality TV personality Kim Kardashian dominated the media in the summer of 2011. In reporting, this means that titillation, hysteria, extremism, and fear rule the day. Heck, I think that more people discovered who I was because I lost my temper on the air on August 8, 2011, delivering a two-minute shouted rant against our corrupt political system than from my previous seventeen years of calmer journalism.

This attention-based media industry is paid for by none other than the vampire industries that dominate our politics. The same groups that fund our politicians also buy commercials on the major media networks. According to the Project for Excellence in Journalism, in 2010 Fox News, MSNBC, and CNN had aggregate revenues of $3.5 billion. During 2012, Republican and Democratic groups, either the parties directly or outside groups affiliated with one of the major parties, will spend $5 to $7 billion on the presidential race alone. While it's not impossible to maintain journalistic independence or cover issue areas that are at odds with both parties, with this funding stream paying the bills, the incentives are stacked against the journalists that want to do this.

Islands of Journalists in an Ocean of PR

The media has been further weakened by the rise of public relations representatives, who do in media what lobbyists do in politics. The change has been dramatic. According to ProPublica, an independent nonprofit news website, "In 1980 there were about 0.45 PR workers per 100,000 population compared with 0.36 journalists. In 2008 there were 0.90 PR people per 100,000 compared to 0.25 journalists." So while the number of journalists fell by a third, the number of public relations professionals hired to influence them tripled. The result is overburdened journalists with less time for each story, surrounded by PR reps, paid to be biased, who offer journalists cherry-picked facts, sources sympathetic to their clients, and sometimes entire written articles or filmed news segments ready for the journalist to put out under his or her own name.

Thought for Sale

Even if journalists are under more pressure than ever, can't we still rely on the academics and other qualified experts who give interviews to explain what's really going on and recommend alternatives? Unfortunately, as mentioned earlier, these experts are also vulnerable to the money of the greedy bastards. For example, as part of the campaign to pass its health care reform legislation, the White House had the US Department of Health and Human Services contract with MIT health care economist Jonathan Gruber to author analyses favorable to the bill. As documented in Huffington Post by Jane Hamsher, founder of the Firedoglake.com news website, Gruber's hired opinions were touted in Ron Brownstein's article in *The Atlantic*. Then White House and congressional Democrats sent seventy-one separate emails to the press pointing to Gruber as a seemingly objective source, without disclosing that Gruber was on the payroll of the people backing the bill—and, in fact, was hired as a public contractor and paid with taxpayer money. Many senators and House members used Gruber's work to justify their legislation. The article was also referenced on President Obama's 2012 election site in a blog post.

When it comes to using money to shape public opinion, though, hiring an individual expert is just the beginning. Some vampire industries attempt to sway entire areas of scientific research to change the public's perception. The Carbon Brief, an online scientific-fact-checking organization, looked at nine hundred scientific studies challenging the theory of global warming, and found that 90 percent of them that seemed to disprove the theory were funded indirectly by Exxon Mobil Corporation. As the ZME Science blog explained, "You don't have to convince people that climate change isn't happening—all you have to do is cast some doubt on that, and people will no longer be certain, and this is a strategy that has been successfully tested by tobacco companies, almost at the same level. . . . A confused public is much, much better than a public who is against you."

Next, Lawmakers (Don't) Write the Bills

While many people assume that senators and representatives personally oversee the writing of the bills they propose and the negotiation of changes in committee, in fact, the process is too technical and detailed for busy legislators to handle. Major bills often run to thousands of pages. It takes skilled staff members to manage this kind of complexity, and the more complex it grows, the more the system perpetuates itself: the longer and more confusing bills are, the more legislators must hire outsiders to manage them.

When the Health Care Reform Bill was being written, Senator Max Baucus chaired the Senate Finance Committee, the main body charged with writing the bill. He selected as the main staffer on the health care overhaul a woman named Liz Fowler, who wrote the government report on which the final legislation was based. Fowler was the former head lobbyist for multibillion-dollar health insurance company WellPoint. After the bill passed, Baucus personally thanked her for putting together the bill. So it is literally true that the Health Care Reform Bill that required Americans to buy health insurance without addressing the outrageous price rigging in the industry was written by the erstwhile vice president of a private health insurance company.

This kind of arrangement is all too common. Politicians defend it by saying that the health insurance executive—or drug company executive, banking executive, energy company executive, media company executive, or military defense executive—understands the issue better than anybody in the government. So how could our legislators *possibly* write the laws when they don't even understand the industry? They *have to* defer to the industry lobbyist, who writes the legislation and presents it to a receptive lawmaker. This is how it came to be, for example, that Julie Chon, a former J. P. Morgan finance analyst working in then Connecticut senator Chris Dodd's office wrote the banking regulation that would affect J. P. Morgan.

It's not impossible that a lobbyist hired by a congressperson could shed the perspective developed while working for his or her corporate employer—namely, what's good for the industry?—and focus instead on duty to the American people.

Even a conflicted doctor paid on the fee-for-service model who still puts the patient ahead of his or her own personal gain can at least expect lifetime employment as a doctor. A congressional staffer hired to write a given piece of legislation knows that the job may well end when the legislation ends, and when it ends, the lucrative work will still be in lobbying. According to the Center for Responsive Politics, 129 former lobbyists are working in "critically important staff positions" in the 112th Congress, up from sixty in the 111th. On the flip side, the Center also reports that, of the 120 former members of the 111th Congress, about 50 percent now work for a lobbying firm or client. How much can you afford to ignore your old boss when he's likely to be your boss again next year?

Finally, the Lawmakers Vote

Once the bills are written and negotiations end, it is a lawmaker's job to represent his or her constituents when voting. But if politicians lose their jobs, they have no constituents to represent.

So they are under two pressures at once: to satisfy the people who elected them to carry out reforms, and to get elected again, which requires money from greedy bastards who often profit by preventing reform. The lawmakers pitch soaring ideas and goals, raising our hopes, then backpedal to keep the campaign contributions coming.

You could see this tension when the pharmaceutical industry cut a secret deal with the White House during the health care reform debate. The *Los Angeles Times* reported that the industry agreed to support health care reform legislation if the government would agree that health care reform would not include any further competition on drug prices. In particular, according to *News Hour,* drug companies agreed to pay $80 million toward the price of prescription drugs not already covered in the Medicare Part D benefits (the so-called "doughnut hole") in exchange for a guarantee that Medicare would not be allowed to negotiate for lower prices on behalf of its patients or to import less expensive drugs from Canada.

The Obama administration denied there was a secret agreement, but when a revised bill was made available to the public, it contained exactly the terms that the *Los Angeles Times* had described in its account of the secret deal. Later, in Finance Committee negotiations, Senator Tom Carper of Delaware defended the deal, saying that Congress had a moral obligation to respect it. Huh? Why, other than this "moral obligation," did legislators agree? The deal had something in it for the legislators, as alluded to by Carper and later confirmed in *The Hill*, the daily newspaper of Congress. The health care industry agreed to fund political advertisements in districts where Democrats were vulnerable in the upcoming 2010 midterm election. Here was the formula for the secret deal, which indeed made it into the final legislation: the drug makers kept their rigged profits, the legislators kept their jobs, and the taxpayers paid both of their bills. Billions go to paying for overpriced drugs instead of improving health. It was classic greedy bastard.

The need to raise funds for the next election is a constant pressure on politicians at every level, from the start of their careers through every major decision they make. My grandfather Frank was mayor of our town, Saranac Lake, New York (population: 5,041). He helped me understand that if you want to become a politician, the single most important relationships you have are with your local banker, insurance agent, and real estate companies—that is, with the business community—because they provide the most money to local candidates. At the federal level, for example, in 2008, so-called FIRE industries (finance, insurance, and real estate) paid for more than 20 percent of all campaign expenses, as documented by the Center for Responsive Politics.

I thought of this when I read how Representative Blake Farenthold, a Tea Party candidate who won in 2010 in a heavily Democratic district in south Texas, described the challenge he was receiving from Tea Party Republicans who believed that he hadn't proved himself conservative enough. "The 2012 primary," he told the *New York Times*, "started the day I took office. There is this constant pressure for fund-raising. I mean, you're always worried about who is going to run against you, but I am willing to stand up for what I believe." But which is it? What happens when a politician has to choose? Do you compete for fund-raising or stand up for what you believe? We would all like to think that campaigning and fund-raising are an occasional break that representatives take from the real work of government, which is passing laws based on the needs of their constituents. But there are constant demands to reverse the two and make voting on bills into a means of raising money for your next campaign.

The financial incentives to vote with the greedy bastards extend beyond political careers. Politicians who are sympathetic to major industries are often hired by those industries once their political work is done. This is essentially a deferred bribe. For example, after the financial crisis, when the Senate debated a new bill to regulate the secret derivatives market, Democrats split. The conservative "Blue Dog" caucus of Democrats supported the weak bill, while liberal Democrat Russ Feingold of Wisconsin voted against the bill because it was not strong enough. After the party was trounced by the Republicans in the midterms, roughly half the Blue Dog Democrats fled Capitol Hill to become high-priced lobbyists. For instance, conservative Democratic congressman Harold Ford Jr. of Tennessee took a $1 million salary at Morgan Stanley, one of the banking companies that had benefitted from his votes.

Republicans got in on the action too. Senator Judd Gregg of New Hampshire, who had argued that the new regulations would turn America into a socialist state and that the bill's name should be changed from the Dodd-Frank Wall Street Reform and Consumer Protection Act to the "Expansion-of-Government-for-Making-Us-More-Like-Europe Act," later became an "international adviser" at Goldman Sachs, the finance industry giant that makes billions of dollars from unregulated derivatives. (Question: How could a bill to restore the capital requirements that we'd had for decades possibly be against America's capitalist values?)

By contrast, Senator Feingold objected to the bill because it didn't do enough to regulate the financial industry. Upon losing his seat that November, he found work as a college professor, making a fraction of what the greedy bastards could offer their supporters. While protecting the derivatives market from regulation ensured pro-secrecy candidates a form of deferred compensation—not just campaign contributions but also money in their personal bank accounts and lasting postpolitics careers—I estimate that voting to end the secrecy of the derivatives market cost Russ Feingold personally at least $750,000 per year. He voted against secrecy anyway, but not many senators did.

When it comes to influencing legislators' votes, nothing is more powerful than the threat of cutting off whatever resource an industry supplies to voters. Brooksley Born, chair of the Commodity Futures Trade Commission from 1996 to 1999, a small agency charged with regulating futures markets, saw the danger of the "swaps" market long before the financial collapse of 2008 and warned the CFTC to regulate it before problems snowballed. Michael Greenberger, former CFTC director of trading and markets, told the 2009 PBS *Frontline* program "The Warning" that when Born proposed the new rules, which would have increased visibility and price integrity for the investment banks selling CDO monster bonds, then deputy secretary of the Treasury Larry Summers called to tell her to stop. Summers had thirteen bankers in his office at that minute with a lot to lose if her rules were put into effect. As Greenberger recollected, Summers told Born that all the bankers agreed that regulating "swaps" would "cause the worst financial crisis since the end of World War II." Those bankers had the leverage to say: stop what you want to do, or the system will go down and the voters won't forgive your party for decades.

Ten years later, after a series of financial crises like those Born had warned about, banksters were still using the same threats to protect their profits. Sheila Bair, chair of the FDIC from 2006 to 2011, told the *New York Times Magazine* as her term was ending, "They would say, 'You have to do this or the system will go down.' If I heard that once, I heard it a thousand times. 'Citi is systemic, you have to do this.' No analysis, no meaningful discussion. It was very frustrating."

If an industry controls something that people believe they must have, then the industry can threaten to take it away and pin the blame on the politicians: "If you regulators don't back down, we'll have gas lines again, and those found responsible will go the way of Jimmy Carter. . . ." And while it's not actually the case that the CEO of Exxon controls all the oil, or that the CEO of UnitedHealthcare controls all access to health insurance, or that the CEO of J. P. Morgan personally controls all the money, these powerful executives influence assets far greater than even their own companies. This special privilege gives that CEO the ability to walk into room and say, in effect, "If you don't give me what I want, I can meaningfully disrupt the flow of something that your constituents can't live without." In that situation, it's very difficult for a politician to do anything but hand over the keys.

If we start from the wishes of the public and follow them through the political system to the laws and regulations that result, we discover an all-too-familiar story. There are greedy bastards waiting at every turn, strapping politicians into a system designed to do their bidding. In the end, just as banks are failing to serve the account holders who trust them with their money, and just as the health care industry is failing to give its patients better health, and just as the energy industry is failing to give its customers clean domestic energy, and just as the education system is failing to help its students learn to learn, so is the political system failing to serve the citizens of the country that President Abraham Lincoln, in the Gettysburg Address, called "government by the people, for the people." At each step, an opaque process hides opportunities for politicians to sell the concerns and rights of their constituents for their own gain—or at least to protect their own jobs.

Read about a thousand of these examples, and you will find in every one a breach of the essential values of VICI: visibility, integrity, choice, and interests. The duped American people don't understand the price they are paying. The interests of the legislators, professional experts, and the others who were supposed to serve the public were instead aligned against them. The apparent choices were really no choice at all, and all of this manipulation was possible because there was not enough visibility: it's so hard to see how the system actually works.

The Real Price of Rigged Politics

Do we understand the full cost of our bought political system? The most obvious price we pay when vampire industries buy political influence is a greedy-bastard appetizer platter of outright waste and theft. Look at military funding. Defense contractors and their lobbyists have waged a multiyear campaign to build an alternative engine for the F-35 fighter jet, even though the original engine works well. The Pentagon has said it does not want the alternative engine—even Defense Secretary Robert Gates called it "costly and unnecessary"— but, astoundingly, in 2011 the House authorized money for it anyway. Why? Because the defense industry has the lobbying power to demand that the government buy its products whether America needs them or not.

As reported by *Politico* in 2011, the lobbying blitz to turn the House victory into a piece of signed legislation was enormous: "13 different lobbying firms, plus each contractor's in-house lobbyists, are engaging lawmakers on the engine issue—focusing on the defense authorization and appropriations bills in which the engine debate will most likely be decided. . . . This year, there are 75 lobbyists working on defense issues at the firms engaged in the second-engine showdown, of whom at least 56—or 75 percent—are former congressional staffers or executive branch officials. Of those, at least 33 are registered to work on the engine issue specifically."

A second cost of a political system that has become a vampire industry is that our legislators must speak out of both sides of their mouths—one side to their constituents, the other to their corporate sponsors. Reasonable men wind up talking and acting like idiots. For example, Republican congressman Mike Pence of Indiana argued admirably that "if we are going to put our fiscal house in order, everything has to be on the table. We have to be willing to look at domestic spending, we have to be able to look at entitlements, and we have to look at defense." Then he turned around and supported funding for the "costly and unnecessary" second F-35 engine.

A third expense is that even problems we know how to solve, with solutions that have won bipartisan support, can't be implemented. The derivatives market is still unregulated, as I've described, even though the champions of banking deregulation, from Alan Greenspan to Larry Summers to President Clinton, have admitted that the financial deregulation of 1999–2000 was a mistake.

Americans are still paying to send our best jobs to China, and paying through military spending three times the posted price for a gallon of gas, not to mention the untold price in environmental damage. The health insurance industry still has its almost unique antitrust exemption, even though Republicans and Democrats alike have spoken out against legal price fixing. The for-profit colleges are still luring our young people to take on reckless loans guaranteed by taxpayers like you and me. Even after the journalistic revelations and the expressions of outrage, it all continues. The vampires still have their teeth sunk deep into America.

But the worst consequence of our rigged political system is the way it effects even the best industries on which we depend—not just the giant vampires but also many smaller industries as well. Let's look more closely at military contractors. As Dean Baker told me on *Radio Free Dylan*, the Defense Department now resembles a trough where every pig "comes running in to get their share." It begins with privatization: contractors lobby the government to outsource more and more military business from the government to—surprise, surprise—them. In the case of intelligence agencies, according to the book *Spies for Hire: The Secret World of Intelligence Outsourcing* by Tim Shorrock, "Over the past decade, contracting for America's spy agencies has grown into a $50 billion industry that eats up seven of every ten dollars spent by the US government on its intelligence services. Today, unbeknownst to most Americans, agencies once renowned for their prowess in analysis, covert operations, electronic surveillance, and overhead reconnaissance outsource many of their core tasks."

In many cases, the same officials who used to work for government simply move to the private sector to do the very same work—at two or three times the pay. "Nearly every [military contactor] has sought out former high-ranking intelligence and national security officials as both managers and directors," Shorrock explained. Author Janine Wedel, a professor of international commerce and policy at the George Mason University School of Public Policy in Fairfax, Virginia, has tracked these trends and shown in her book *Shadow Elite* how they operate to pervert the objectives of US purchasing priorities.

One example is Michael Chertoff, former Homeland Security secretary. After he left government service, he was lucky enough to set up his own consulting firm, the Chertoff Group, while at the same time appearing as a security expert in the media. One of his clients was a company called Rapiscan, which makes the full body scanners used by the Transportation Security Administration when checking people in at the airport.

Chertoff used his position as a former security official to convince the American people that full-body airport scanners were effective. Chertoff appeared frequently as a commentator on the television news—nearly a dozen times after a terrorist attempted to bomb a plane on Christmas, in 2009. He wrote an op-ed for the *Washington Post* touting full-body systems, without disclosing that Rapiscan was one of his clients. Chertoff was variously introduced as a security expert or former cabinet official, but not generally as an unofficial spokesperson for Rapiscan. He got his political allies to continue putting up taxpayer money for the devices he was pushing as a "security" matter.

It isn't obvious that Rapiscan devices do anything except enrich special interests. The General Accountability Office (GAO) did a study in 2010 on these scanners, and reported that "it remains unclear whether" they would have detected any weapons used in the Christmas bombing scheme. The US Airline Pilots Association told its members not to submit to screenings used by these devices. But Chertoff, who hired eleven former Homeland Security officials to work in his consulting firm, successfully persuaded the government to purchase these scanners anyway. Money for them was included in Obama's 2009 stimulus, and then another $25 million was used by the TSA to buy more scanners in January 2010. In total, the government allowed the TSA to spend $173 million on the equipment—not a bad return for however much Rapiscan paid Chertoff.

What does Chertoff care? The media continued to call him a security expert and a former cabinet official instead of what he was—a body scanner salesman. Former and current government officials continued to work to appropriate our money for his allies. No wonder that Dean Baker advised me to "think about the health care system in the way we think about the Defense Department": as a corrupted entity, hawking services we don't need at prices we can't afford.

How to Break the Stranglehold

Instead of Lincoln's ideal of government by the people, for the people, where the public tells the legislators what it needs and the legislators codify those needs into law through open debate and group problem solving (which depends on VICI values), we drift ever closer to government funded by the lobbyists, for the greedy bastards, and directly at our expense. Any of our major industries yields similar examples of greedy bastards rigging both policy de-

The Unholy Alliance

Every choice to align the interests of politicians with everyone else by eliminating money and gerrymandering and closed primaries enhances productive policy making; every choice to breach it destroys it.

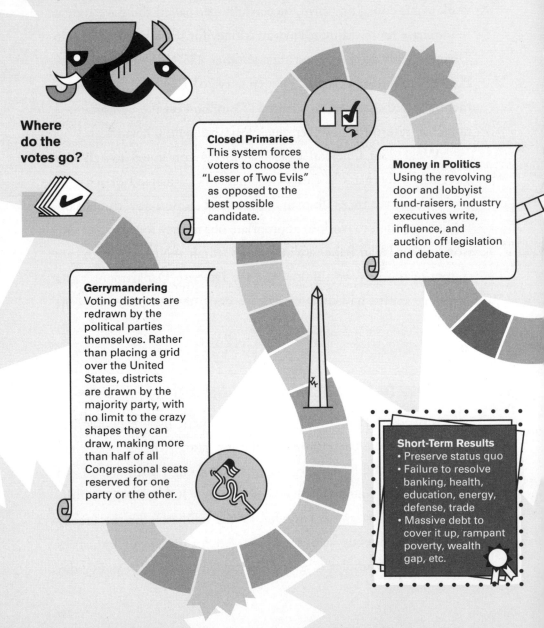

Where do the votes go?

Closed Primaries
This system forces voters to choose the "Lesser of Two Evils" as opposed to the best possible candidate.

Money in Politics
Using the revolving door and lobbyist fund-raisers, industry executives write, influence, and auction off legislation and debate.

Gerrymandering
Voting districts are redrawn by the political parties themselves. Rather than placing a grid over the United States, districts are drawn by the majority party, with no limit to the crazy shapes they can draw, making more than half of all Congressional seats reserved for one party or the other.

Short-Term Results
• Preserve status quo
• Failure to resolve banking, health, education, energy, defense, trade
• Massive debt to cover it up, rampant poverty, wealth gap, etc.

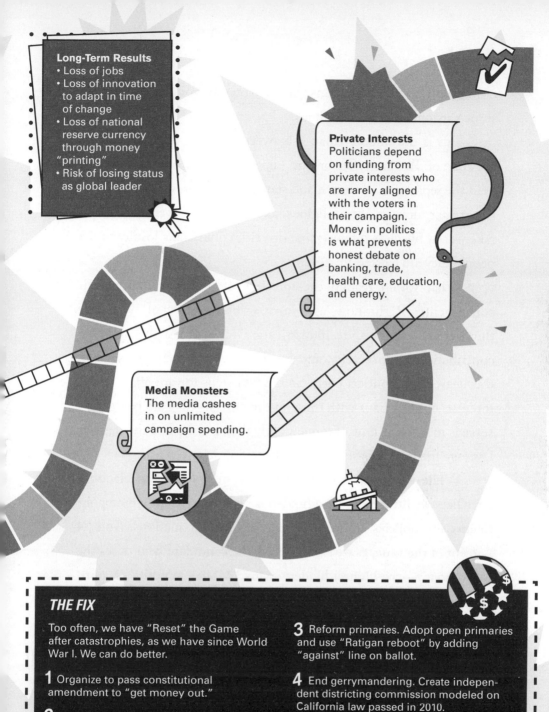

Long-Term Results
• Loss of jobs
• Loss of innovation to adapt in time of change
• Loss of national reserve currency through money "printing"
• Risk of losing status as global leader

Private Interests
Politicians depend on funding from private interests who are rarely aligned with the voters in their campaign. Money in politics is what prevents honest debate on banking, trade, health care, education, and energy.

Media Monsters
The media cashes in on unlimited campaign spending.

THE FIX

Too often, we have "Reset" the Game after catastrophies, as we have since World War I. We can do better.

1 Organize to pass constitutional amendment to "get money out."

2 Advocate for Congress to pass a campaign fund-raising tax of 100 percent.

3 Reform primaries. Adopt open primaries and use "Ratigan reboot" by adding "against" line on ballot.

4 End gerrymandering. Create independent districting commission modeled on California law passed in 2010.

5 The one thing everyone can do starting today: demand government visibility, to expose misaligned interests and hypocrisy.

cisions and business decisions for their own ongoing benefit using some version of these techniques.

This is the unholy alliance between business and state. Since the time of Thomas Jefferson and James Madison, America has upheld the separation of church and state. Today, however, we find that the greater threat is not a religious takeover of the government but a takeover by business interests that overrides politicians' loyalty to the people they are elected to serve.

What would realign the interests of politicians with their constituents? Right now, as I've described, politicians who ally themselves with vampire industries are rewarded with campaign contributions, job security, and lucrative private sector jobs when they leave their political posts. So the first steps toward aligning the interests of politicians with those of the citizens they are pledged to serve is to stop the flow of money. Only then can we end the massive leverage the greedy bastards use to keep politicians in line.

While we appear to hold elections, in practice our elections have become little more than fund-raising competitions where politicians and policies are sold off in privately run auctions. And 94 percent of the time, as we saw in 2008, the candidate who raises the most money—the highest bidder—wins. "Money in politics is pure, unadulterated corruption," stated lobbyist Jimmy Williams. "It's not that all lobbyists or politicians are bad. It's that they are operating in a system whose foundation is built completely on how much money is raised for or against you. We have amended the US constitution twice with regard to liquor but not once with regard to the buying and selling of our politicians. Something is wrong with this picture and there is only one way to fix it."

Williams, myself, and millions of Americans agree: if you ban money in politics, the interests of lawmakers and the law-making process will once again align with constituents, and politicians can go forward with the work of helping those constituents realize their potential, rather than focusing on raising money for their own re-election.

REFORM CAMPAIGN FINANCE. I think almost every voter who sees how political campaigns are financed would agree that the system needs fixing. The question is how to do it fairly. A constitutional amendment could make it illegal for any politician to accept direct or indirect private money or support ever again. Simply, elected officials would be prevented from taking private money, period.

Here's a rough draft of the amendment I'm fighting for to get money out of politics:

> No person, corporation, or business entity, domestic or foreign, shall be allowed to contribute money, directly or indirectly, to any candidate for federal office or to contribute money on behalf of or opposed to any type of campaign for federal office. Notwithstanding any other provision of law, campaign contributions to candidates for federal office shall not constitute speech of any kind as guaranteed by the US constitution or any amendment to the US constitution. Congress shall set forth a holiday for the purposes of voting for candidates for federal office.

Efforts like this have failed many times for many reasons, and it is clear no politician or person or group can do this alone. As Representative John Yarmuth of Kentucky described to me, money in politics is like a suicide-bomber vest that every politician must wear. If any one politician tries to remove the money vest, he or she blows up. The only way to remove money from politics safely is if every politician is forced to remove their money vests at the same time.

But a constitutional amendment can take years to ratify. Women's voting rights took more than seventy years from start to finish. Our country simply doesn't have that kind of time. As an emergency measure, what if we imposed a fund-raising tax? Imagine, a 100 percent tax on all political fund-raising: for every dollar you raise, you have to pay a dollar. That money could be used to finance federal elections, or for that matter, reduce the deficit or even feed poor children. The tax would mean that if a well-moneyed candidate like then Senator Barack Obama wants to raise $740 million, he would pay a $740 million tax—that could go to a public campaign fund for his potential opponents or to reduce the deficit.

In 1998, the state of Arizona attempted something along these lines with the Citizens Clean Election Act, which tried to give more money to candidates who accepted public financing if a candidate with private money spent more than the cap for public funding. However, the US Supreme Court, in a decision that must have cheered greedy bastards everywhere, struck down this provision of the law 5–4, arguing that it limited the free speech of the wealthy candidate. Still, we can hope that in the future the minority view, expressed in a dissent by Justice Elena Kagan, will find one more vote: "Except in a world gone topsy-turvy," she wrote, "additional campaign speech and electoral competition is not a First Amendment injury." In other words, we need a political system with *more* real debate and competition, not less. Otherwise, what's the point of democracy?

BLOCK THE REVOLVING DOOR. Campaign finance reform would start to realign politicians' financial interests so that they couldn't be so easily paid to ignore voters' needs. We must also block the revolving door that brings politicians quickly and lucratively into the private sector as lobbyists or working directly for the vampire industries that benefitted from their votes. There needs to be a seven-year cooling-off period for all lawmakers, staffers, and regulators from working in any related industry or lobbying their former colleagues, to prevent this form of delayed bribery.

While this might sound draconian, ask yourself do you really think we are getting high-quality public servants with the current incentive structure? I am betting that we would get much more capable government officials once we hindered their ability to get rich off their service. To make this work, we must place the legal onus on politicians to disclose every possible breach and potential conflict of interest, be it an invite to a BBQ hosted by lobbyists or arranging to get a politician's nephew a job with a contractor. This information could be updated weekly on open-source searchable databases—there is no shortage of smart, patriotic Americans who can take it from there. Then, if politicians are found negligent of material disclosure, they need to be fined, fired, and possibly jailed. It is a sad state of affairs we have today when corporations, which clearly don't work for us, are forced to disclose more to the public than politicians are.

END GERRYMANDERING. If the United States were one congressional district, it would be 35 percent Independent, 33 percent Democrat, and 32 percent Republican. So why is it then that nearly all 435 Congressional districts look nothing like the makeup of

America? Congressional districts are devised by the political parties themselves. Rather than simply placing a grid over the map of the Unites States, districts are drawn by the majority party with no limit on the crazy shapes they can draw on the map. The result is that more than half are configured as safe seats reserved essentially for one party. Talk about a breach of political choice!

The experience of Representative Glenn Nye is sadly typical. He told me, "As a candidate for Congress in 2008 [win] and again in 2010 [loss], I heard consistently from all kinds of people at all types of events how they want their representative to work with both parties and focus on common sense ideas that help strengthen the economy and solve practical problems. Yet when most people go to the polls they never get that choice. As most successful candidates have only a primary challenge to worry about, they are naturally driven to focus on issues appealing to one side of the political spectrum, and increasingly so." The result is that we hear an enormous amount about the issues that divide us—abortion, gay marriage, and so on—yet rarely do we reach consensus on critical issues because of greedy bastards' influence on politicians. We see this every day from the jobs debate to energy and education. For example, if districts were more balanced, even if voters did not always get their first choice of candidates, officials would have to listen carefully to all points of view and focus more on shared interests. As Representative Nye said, "Changing election financing won't fix that. Only nonpartisan districting will."

In 2010, the state of California attempted to resolve this problem by passing Proposition 20, which took the power to write district lines away from the elected state legislators and gave it to a newly formed commission. That panel of fourteen is made up of five Democrats, five Republicans, and four voters with no party affiliation—and they exclusively hold the power to draw district lines. Imagine this system on all 435 districts coupled with a ban on money and you could be on your way to a Congress that looks acts and thinks like America instead of the greedy bastards who run the place now.

SAY NO TO THE LESSER-OF-TWO-EVILS VOTING. The coauthors of *Renewing the American Dream: A Citizen's Guide for Restoring Our Competitive Advantage,* Frank Islam, George Muñoz, and Ed Crego, argued to me in the hallways of NBC before the 2010 midterm elections for including an "against line" on our electoral ballots. On the first line, voters would choose between the two candidates. On the second line, they would vote on whether the winner should take office or whether they would prefer a new election.

After I shared this idea with journalist Mickey Kaus, he expanded on it in a blog on the *Newsweek* website: "Call it Instant Recall voting," Kaus wrote. "No longer would you be stuck with the two turkeys picked by the highly polarized primary electorates of the Democrats and Republicans. Voters could reject them both without having, at the same time, to settle on the candidate they actually wanted. Do you have to have a new boyfriend in order to break up with your old boyfriend? I didn't think so."

The Ratigan Reboot, as Kaus named it, could give all voters the chance to force politicians to listen to everyone, and not just to the radical fringe of the party that controls the district.

As Kaus wrote: "In a gerrymandered district—say 70% Democratic—an extreme left candidate can win office by getting 50% of the Democratic primary vote, or 35% of all voters. In a Ratigan Recall election, that would win him the primary, *and* the general—but he'd also have to survive a Reboot vote in which the 34% of voters who voted against him in the primary might join with the 30% of voters who are Republican to deny him the office. Better not be *too* extreme."

END THE LEFTY-RIGHTY FACADE. What frustrates me the most is how we have gotten stuck with two monopoly parties that control the choices we receive, which is barely any choice at all. Their monopoly limits not just who represents us but also the issues they discuss. Our political debate is the rhetorical equivalent of professional wrestling, covered profitably by cable news channels; fake competitions designed for the cameras. Meanwhile, our serious challenges fester. As we wait for the next smackdown—Are the Republicans up? Are the Democrats down?—the media "covers" this contrived clash, pretending that the shift in power from one party to the other would address our biggest problems. We need media that *uncovers* what every chapter of this book shows: that both Democrats and Republicans give away vast amounts of taxpayer money to greedy bastards; they just go about it differently. As a result, like any other vampire industry, politics has become an exercise in ruthless self-preservation, a monopoly that exists mainly to keep existing when its productive value has faded away.

END THE BOGUS POLITICAL DEBATES. In this time of extraordinarily fast change, we desperately need a government to encourage structural transitions that will bring about adaptation, so we can dig our way out of the mountain of debt that's burying us, solve our biggest problem and create jobs. Instead we have a two-party system that works *against debating the hard questions and destroying the vampires.* As Senator Tom Coburn of Oklahoma observed on our show, "Republicans are trying to protect the Republican brand, Democrats are trying to protect the Democrat brand, and what we don't have is enough statesmen trying to solve the problems of our country." Consider these three bogus, brand-protecting debates that I wish we would never hear again:

BOGUS DEBATE NO. 1: BIG GOVERNMENT VERSUS SMALL GOVERNMENT

Republicans argue that government ought to be smaller. Democrats disagree. But the entire argument is a distraction because it misses the key point: there is nothing inherently good or bad about an organization's size. I'm in the television news business. Am I in favor of big television news organizations or small ones? Neither. The real issue is how big an organization do I need in order to do a good job? And the answer depends on what job I'm trying to do, which evolves over time. If I'm trying to create a news podcast where I talk with experts in different fields, then I need a little closet to record in, a telephone, some microphones, a few other pieces of equipment, and a couple of staff members to run the machinery and help me recruit guests. For that particular job, a small organization fits the bill just fine. But if I'm trying to cover the Super Bowl, I need a lot of equipment and a pretty big staff, don't I? The same goes for the organization called government. As conservative *New York Times* columnist David Brooks put it, "The best way to measure government is not by volume, but by what you might call the Achievement Test. Does a given policy arouse energy, foster skills, spur social mobility, and help people transform their lives?"

The debate should not be "Government, big or small?" The debate should be: "We're saddled with a bought government. How do we get rid of the greedy bastards and build an aligned and effective government?" Will the Republican dream of the smallest, cheapest government possible be strong enough to break the grip of the vampire industries? I don't think so. Will a big, corrupt, redundant bureaucracy be flexible enough to adapt to our changing times? I doubt it. So politicians, please, *shut up* about big and small. Show up tomorrow for a new debate. Make your case about what will do the job. And to whomever wins, let's say, Please get down to solving problems.

BOGUS DEBATE NO. 2: LOWER TAXES VERSUS HIGHER TAXES

This debate is doubly fake. You have the Democrats contending that taxes are lower than any time in recent history, and the Republicans insisting that we need to reduce taxes further. In reality, both parties have effectively introduced massive new taxes—but off the balance sheet, where they can't be seen. As I've explained, the banking bailout was an indirect tax increase. Quantitative easing—money printing—is an indirect tax increase: it gives the government more money to play with while reducing the buying power of the ordinary American, as the glut of money causes commodity inflation on everything from gas to food. Tolerating vampire industries yields an endless series of trillion-dollar tax increases, because it benefits the politicians while requiring all citizens to pay more for less, and from fewer sources, too.

Every price distortion is effectively a tax. When an industry uses its power to fix a price artificially high, that extra amount you're paying is no different from an extra tax added at the register. When a price is held artificially low, so we buy more of it, like gasoline or corn, then it turns out we're asked to cover the whole price later in paying for externalities such as environmental damage, lost jobs, and harm to our health. The fact that we don't pay these secret taxes on April 15 doesn't change their impact on our bank accounts and our lives.

But even if we're talking about old-fashioned visible taxes, the debate is still bogus. The questions should not be, "Do we have a high income tax or a low income tax?" and "Do we tax the rich or the poor?" Instead we should be asking, "Given that the tax code is part of the government and the purpose of government is to serve the people and help the United States to thrive, what tax code does that best? What tax code encourages us to invest in this country, to solve our most pressing problems in energy, health care, and education in ways that create good jobs for hardworking Americans?" The problem is that we are in urgent need of great American innovation, but this takes more time and much harder work than grabbing easy money while no one is looking. We need a tax code that discourages short-term greed (in the forms of high-frequency trading, commodity speculation, extraction) and encourages investors here and abroad to invest in the United States for the long term and for the highest value.

I don't claim to have all the answers on this one, but it seems to me that if we agree that there's nothing wrong with getting rich, and that we want to encourage people to use their wealth in ways that are productive, not extractive, then that's what our tax code should do. Tax spending—consumption—rather than income, and let the tax code reward long-term investors. If you find a way to use your computer to extract money from the stock market in a few seconds, you should be taxed very high. If you commit your money for years, launch a business, and build something new that others can use, you should be taxed low.

A well-run country is like any well-run business: greedy, but long-term greedy. We need a tax code that will bring out the long-term greedy and in the process align the interests of Americans.

BOGUS DEBATE NO. 3: MORE DEBT OR LESS DEBT

Debt is a serious problem for a nation, just as bleeding is a serious problem for an injured person. But controlling bleeding does not necessarily do anything to address the cause of the injury or illness that caused the bleeding. Talking about debt endlessly distracts from figuring out what matters: what caused the bleeding and how to stop it.

Whenever you hear a politician—Republican, Independent, or Democrat—engaging in any of these three bogus debates, you can be sure that there is something else, some vampire industry, that he doesn't want you to know about. Maybe he doesn't want you asking about the bank bailout, which added trillions to our national debt. Maybe he doesn't want you talking about health care spending, which will swamp any attempt at cost cutting if it's not controlled. Maybe he hopes you won't notice our astonishingly wasteful energy industry. But rest assured that he'll keep harping on the debt as long as it distracts you from the unholy alliance between business and government. Because while you're distracted by the political smackdowns between parties, he can go on being a greedy bastard.

Can the People Win?

The weapons that the vampire industries use to cripple democracy can also be turned against them. The disingenuous debates can be replaced with genuine problem solving. The fragmented media can never be put back together, but it offers new tools for revealing the so-called experts who have been bought, as well as for renewing debate that is not measured in whether the Democrats or the Republicans win. The two-party wrestling match can be preempted by new alliances and broad-based coalitions that can merge and align to address individual challenges. Let's look at a recent example that offers a glimmer of what may come.

As part of the government's response to the financial crisis of 2008, the Federal Reserve lent out over $1 trillion. From 2007 to 2009, its balance sheet grew from $800 billion in plain-vanilla government securities to over $2 trillion in exotic commercial debt and odd credit instruments. The explanation heard endlessly in the major media was that these were "emergency loans" by which the government "rescued" us from financial meltdown. But where exactly was all that taxpayer money going? No one outside the Fed knew, because the bankers weren't saying, and there had never been an independent audit of the Fed in the nearly one hundred years of its existence.

The attempt to learn what the Fed was doing with that enormous amount of money seemed like the kind of well-meaning effort bound to fail in a political system that had become a vampire industry. The Fed hired Linda Robertson, the former chief lobbyist for Enron, to handle a public relations campaign opposing an audit, and gathered "impartial" experts to testify that continued secrecy was necessary.

But a surprising alliance of legislators pushed for an audit. They included Representative Ron Paul, a libertarian from Texas, Senator Bernie Sanders, a socialist from Vermont, and Congressman Alan

Grayson, a firebrand liberal from Florida. In an aggressive Senate hearing, Grayson asked Elizabeth Coleman, the inspector general of the Fed, "Do you know who received that one trillion dollars-plus that the Fed extended and put on its balance sheet since last September? Do you know the identity of the recipients?" Coleman replied, "I do not." As Grayson told me later, "That video has become the most watched congressional video in history," seen by over three million people, "watching in horror, to understand that . . . these un-elected officials could hand out a trillion dollars and not even know who got the money."

To neutralize the credibility of the experts brought in to vouch for the Fed, journalist Ryan Grim at the Huffington Post reported on how the Fed itself funded much of the "independent" macro-economic research on monetary policy that it then used to justify its activities. Grim followed up repeatedly, showing how supposedly disinterested experts were on the payroll of the Fed. A coalition of grassroots leaders such as Jane Hamsher of Firedoglake, economist Dean Baker, Yves Smith, and the Campaign for Liberty, a group committed to the constitution, noninterventionist foreign policy, and the free market, kept up a drumbeat in the financial blogs and helped rally the public against the Fed. Tens of thousands of people signed petitions in favor of an audit.

Meanwhile, Bloomberg journalist Mark Pittman sued the Fed to force it to reveal data concerning emergency loans, and the political fight benefitted from the publicity as that case worked its way through the courts. The hot public pressure, along with the focus brought to the process by the network of activists and staffers linked to concerned citizens through both traditional and new media, and constant lobbying of other legislators by Grayson, Paul, and Sanders overcame Fed and Treasury pressure. The emergency lending data were released publicly, spawning hundreds of stories on how the Fed supported hedge funds, banks, and even the wife of the CEO of Morgan Stanley. The door of visibility, the necessary first step in applying the VICI code, had cracked open.

8

It's Just Us

Think of the most powerful state ever known. It had a tradition of laws and representative government, a network of roads, and a system of communications that were marvels of their time. It boasted an urbane culture, prosperous cities, and a military superior to any that had ever been, with technology and engineering far surpassing those of its enemies. Everywhere, people wanted to become its citizens.

I am describing ancient Rome, but the parallels to America are many: in the later years of the Roman Empire, wealth and power were increasingly consolidated in the hands of a few. The military become entangled in more numerous and unprofitable wars. The elites—what today we would call special interests—feuded over the spoils from an extractive economy. Fewer products were manufactured by Romans, and the empire became dependent on grain from North Africa and Western Europe. The people were burdened with heavy taxation and predatory lending. Politics became increasingly corrupt, until only those wealthy enough to pay for part of a local government's budget could win local office. Senators fought one another for power while the economy weakened. The Emperor Nero, last in a long line of emperors stretching back to Augustus, lowered the percentage of silver in the coins he used to pay the military and the special interests on whom his power depended, becoming one of the original money printers. Over decades, the Roman currency, the *dinarii*, became so degraded that other countries stopped using it as the basis for international trade. The resulting fiscal crisis helped to bring down the empire.

America is unlike ancient Rome in many ways, but we are a great power similarly vulnerable to predatory special interests and the threat of financial collapse. As vampire industries exploit their unholy alliance with government to extract capital in all the ways I have described, we are increasingly unable to produce the goods we need for ourselves or to pay our debts. Our government covers up the problem by printing more money. If another country printed money as we do, its currency would decrease in value—look at the diminished value of the Italian lira thousands of years later before it was swallowed into the euro.

So far, while printing US currency has created a speculative rise in global food and energy prices, it has not created a precipitous decline in the buying power of the dollar. As I explained in chapter 2, this is because the dollar has "reserve currency status": since 1945, all the countries of the world have agreed to conduct large international business transactions in our currency. Every country in the world, most notably China, holds dollars in reserve, and when we print more, the result is money printing in other countries. This means that they bear some of the cost of our greedy bastards. In this manner, our money printing actually extracts capital from all countries of the globe, not just America.

But the government keeps printing money, and the pressure on the dollar keeps building. Our government and banks create debt to pay for the unfunded wars in oil-producing countries, and the pressure builds. They create for all of us debt that goes to pay for cleaning up oil spills and other energy disasters, and the pressure builds. They create debt to cover out-of-control Medicare costs, and the pressure builds. They create debt to pay for predatory student loans, and the pressure builds. And when it is all too much and the system begins to falter as it did in the crisis of 2008 or in Europe in 2011, instead of resolving the underlying misalignment of interests creating the debt, the government prints money in bailouts to cover up the problem.

When a reserve currency becomes degraded enough, as happened to the Roman dinarii, other countries find it too costly to conduct their business in that currency and shift to a more reliable one. If the world community abandons the dollar, it will probably switch to a basket of currencies including the Chinese yuan. Our last trick for hiding the ongoing vampire extractions from our economy will be lost, and the once-mighty dollar will collapse like a burst balloon, becoming suddenly, disastrously weaker.

Driving Blind

How can this be true? How can we be heading for economic catastrophe when the United States still looks like a wealthy, productive country capable of growth? While it's true that our recent growth, as measured in gross domestic product, has been *disappointing* compared to growth in earlier decades, it doesn't look like a *catastrophe*. Except, just like our vampire industries, our main gauge for measuring growth has outlived its natural life. As Umair Haque explained on *Radio Free Dylan*, the economic measurement that we call gross domestic product (GDP) was never intended to be used as we use it. It's as if America is a car at night on a country lane, with no headlights to illuminate the road in front of us, no speedometer to tell us how fast we're going, and no odometer to tell us how far we've come. So we stare at the tachometer and hope for the best, but it can't tell us what we need to know. All it tells us is how fast the engine is revving, and we ride on through the night, driving blind. Let me explain.

GDP was invented in the 1930s, when Presidents Herbert Hoover and Franklin Roosevelt were trying to design policies to fight the Great Depression. They needed to know how dire it was out there. Lacking a gauge of national success, the government relied on incomplete statistics such as stock price indexes and freight car loadings. They were driving blind. Then economics Nobel laureate Simon Kuznets came up with a way to measure the flow of money through the economy as a whole. But his method had flaws, which he warned of at the time.

First, it tracked only the flow of money moving among different sectors of the economy, not the creation and sale of actual things such as cars or food. Back then, when we had a mainly industrial economy, most economic activity came from making and selling physical products, so Kuznets felt that the approximation was close enough. The second major problem was that it tended to undercount outside costs, or what economists call externalities. Take these two flaws together today, though, and your measurements of national wealth and welfare are highly misleading.

How misleading? Umair Haque once posted the following economic advice on Twitter: "Hey, you want to boost GDP? Go and break your neighbor's arm." And he's right: if you and I and everyone we know would go out and break just one person's arm, there would be a huge increase in emergency room visits, and the money spent to set all those broken bones and to fill all those prescriptions for painkillers would show up in GDP as new financial flows. But what wouldn't be reflected were the resulting losses: the missed days of work, the lost productivity from those arms immobilized in slings, as well as the harm to national trust and morale caused by this nationwide outbreak of violence.

"GDP is often confused with the measure of wealth, but it's not," Haque told me. "It's often confused with the measure of welfare, but it's not." GDP measures only internal movement. It can tell us how fast the engine is turning over, but not how fast we're going or whether we're getting anywhere. What this means is that we have no way to measure, on a national scale, the difference between productive deals and extractive deals.

Our reliance on a gauge that doesn't work skews our sense of how we're doing as a nation. According to GDP, in the 1990s, as the banksters developed CDO monster bonds and credit default swaps, GDP suggested that productivity accelerated. The United States was back! Only recently have economists figured out the two sources of what looked like a productivity spike: big box stores such as Wal-Mart and computerized finance. These two sectors of the economy, which didn't exist when Kuznets invented GDP, benefitted the most from the Internet boom. But as we've seen, the financial services industry is basically predatory, extracting money rather than producing value, and Wal-Mart is a trading company that specializes in outsourcing American jobs to China. Remove them from GDP, and we can see that the nineties weren't a return to prosperity at all. That decade's seeming prosperity was Wal-Mart and the banksters breaking Americans' arms. And there is still no one stopping them today. According to economist and author Peter Morici, almost half of America's entire GDP growth from 2000 to 2010 came exclusively from banking and insurance.

Now you see how we could be hurtling blindly toward financial catastrophe while thinking things look only discouraging. The reason that most Americans, including economists and journalists, can't tell the difference between extractionism and capitalism is that both create a lot of short-term deals, and that's all the instrument we use to measure our economy can count.

We need a yardstick that measures the difference between good deals and bad deals—between investment on new research to cure disease and tripling the price of an old drug; between education that prepares students for the future and predatory loans that put young people in debt with little to show for it. Replacing GDP in this way might seem impractical, but our competitors are already working on it. In 2011, India announced plans to update GDP for the new century. China revealed that it had tried to institute a new GDP measure from 2004 to 2007, but the effort was bogged down in political infighting. (Just because China has been so useful to greedy American bastards doesn't mean that it doesn't suffer from its own greedy Chinese bastards. Greedy bastardism is a global affliction.)

The Ratigan Hypothesis

Whichever country can develop and implement a tool to make visible the real costs and benefits of its deals will create the visibility it needs to stop rewarding greedy bastards and to align interests. Only the modern tools of digital information make this possible. That country can then do the hard work of becoming as productive as possible for the twenty-first century. What would that take? Four steps, all familiar to readers of this book: (1) we must update our gauge so that we can better tell good deals from bad, (2) get the money out of politics, (3) restore capital requirements across the finance industry, and (4) cancel debt based on idle speculation. The Ratigan Hypothesis is that we are the first generation to be able to use modern communication tools to fix our debt problem without resorting to war.

Today debt begets debt, and we are stuck in an ever more destructive game of Trade a Cup. But where extractionism creates debt, capitalism creates value. When we shift from vampire values to the VICI code, the banking and tax and trade systems will no longer reward speculation. Self-interest will push the banksters—and, in fact, *all* greedy bastards—to get back to making wise investments and valuable products. Trade a Cup will no longer pay, and self-interest will guide Americans back to Make a Cup. We will create higher-quality, less expensive products and services in every industry. We will take the forces of short-term greed that are destroying us and harness them for a long-term-greedy renaissance.

Rage

But remember what comes at the end of the Trade a Cup game: rage. The ferocious rage of those who have been ripped off and deceived for decades. As we restore enough visibility that people begin to understand what has been done to their country—for example, when former finance journalists publish books with provocative titles like *Greedy Bastards*—some of us, out of frustration or a hunger for vengeance, will want to attack not just the vampire industries that must die to make room for the industries of the future but also the individual greedy bastards themselves.

I understand that impulse, but it would be a mistake. In fact, rage is much better channeled into repairing what is broken. I believe that all but the worst of the greedy bastards are soldiers in a bad war. They enlisted with the powerful industries and followed their orders because it is the safest way to preserve their sense of an endangered way of life. Being a greedy bastard is the easiest money, the most direct route to a bigger house, vacations, good schools for the kids, and lots of support to take care of your parents as they get older. That's what the system provides: short-term comfort and security at almost any cost.

But should we blame the soldiers? Is it the right thing to attack them as people? One leader who understood this question was Nelson Mandela, the first black president of South Africa. As a young man, Mandela was an activist who led an aggressive campaign against the apartheid regime, one of the most brutal racially oppressive regimes in history. For his trouble, he spent nearly thirty years in jail. You can imagine that after decades in prison, he had more than enough reason to hate the whites who had lived in luxury off the apartheid system while black South African leaders were imprisoned, tortured, and murdered. But President Mandela refused to divide his country into the good "us," the blacks, and the evil "them," the whites. He found the personal resolve to work with the whites for the good of the country. In his first trip abroad as president, he traveled to Japan and Germany and said, I need you to invest in South Africa, I need you to work with South African bankers, white and black, because we need investment and jobs.

Despite the ongoing problems in South Africa caused by its brutally repressive legacy, including mass poverty, crime, and an AIDS epidemic, the country did not descend into civil war and dictatorship. It has a functional economy, and, gradually, the elected civil leadership of the country is finding ways to solve its housing and jobs problems. Museums dedicated to the memory of racial strife dot South Africa, and a new generation is growing up in a post-apartheid world. This was Mandela's resolve: not to see his country divided into us versus them. He avoided collapse, when collapse was the most probable course. It is possible not to go the way of Rome.

In my experience, there aren't many people who always behave admirably or always behave badly. If you've ever spent a stretch of time with a child—or if you remember being one—you know that children are generous and selfish, kind and cruel, often in the same afternoon. We have all enjoyed the feeling of doing the right thing, and we have all enjoyed the feeling of taking what we want when we want it, no matter how it affects anyone else. Most greedy bastards, given an environment based on VICI values, might make very different choices. So even though there is cause for rage, like Mandela we must find the resolve to live by our values and extend a hand.

I've found that the most productive and successful institutions, from countries to companies, share that resolve. As Dr. John H. Noseworthy, the CEO of the Mayo Clinic, told me in conversation when I visited, "There is no us and them. It's just us." That perspective was once strong in this America. In the decade after the Allied victory in World War II, President Eisenhower had great credibility, and in the political conversation, there was a widely shared feeling that we could set collective goals and reach them: the national highway system, the power grid, and so forth. Of course, there were many groups excluded from the political conversation and from economic opportunity—minorities, women, gays—but even the protest movements that arose on behalf of those groups shared the assumption that there ought to be a common "us" and that everyone could participate.

President Kennedy extended that resolve further, saying that we could dream beyond the infrastructure of the country, all the way to the Moon. Today people often say that if we could put a man on the Moon, why can't we do *x*, *y*, or *z*? But what's missing in America is not the *ability* to do great things but the *resolve* to see the country as one great *us*, to unite to achieve goals that benefit all. I believe that feeling was badly damaged with the betrayals of the 1960s and 1970s—assassinations of our leaders, divisions over the Vietnam War, and the Watergate scandal, among other reasons—and it shifted our mentality to "us versus them." We had hippies versus straights, warmongers versus draft dodgers, blacks versus whites, and a long list of other parallel divisions, many of which persist to this day. American politics became the game of separating people into subgroups in order to help them take things from one another—exploitation for the benefit of "us" at the expense of "them"—and ever since we have been stuck with the infrastructure of the Eisenhower 1950s and the political divisions of the 1960s and 1970s.

Silver Bullets in Our Pockets

If we can stop the greedy bastards from rigging banking, taxes, and trade, and realign industries from health care to politics, what then? What might we be capable of if our energy were plentiful, domestic, and cheap? If our education system prepared all of our children to make great contributions to our fast-changing future, *and* at a fraction of the cost? I know these goals sound far off, and perhaps some even sound impossible, but I've watched the impossible happen for my entire life. I watched the underdog 1980 US Olympic hockey team beat the Russians in Lake Placid, while the jubilant crowd chanted "U-S-A! U-S-A!" I watched Boston College quarterback Doug Flutie connect with a receiver on a game-winning Hail Mary pass in the end zone as time ran out. I've watched talented friends with little in the way of advantages triumph over adversity of many kinds. I know that *capital* really means everything that's possible. I know that American capitalism could again be the engine of impossible success and prosperity.

How can I say that? Haven't there been greedy bastards throughout human history? Yes, but we have never had the means to stand up to them that we have now. The digital age makes VICI enforcement mechanisms possible for the first time ever—and this isn't just a metaphor. We can see the practical differences that digital technologies have made in recent events. Just look at the revolution in 2011 that brought down Hosni Mubarak, the Egyptian president who had ruled for thirty years. As Robert Fisk reported in the *Independent*, "the critical moment came on the evening of 30 January when, it is now clear, Mubarak ordered the Egyptian Third Army to crush the demonstrators in Tahrir Square with their tanks after flying F-16 fighter bombers at low level over the protesters. Many of the senior tank commanders could be seen tearing off their headsets—over which they had received the fatal orders—to use their mobile phones. They were, it now transpires, calling their own military families for advice. Fathers who had spent their lives serving the Egyptian army told their sons to disobey, that they must never kill their own people."

In that moment, when the commanders took off their army-issued headsets and switched to their private cell phones, digital technologies helped them to find a VICI alternative. These technologies can enable us to link ourselves together to solve the problems that concern us most. There is almost always somebody in the digital crowd who can see what is really happening, not what the incumbent powers want us to see. There is someone who has the answer to almost any question, and if there is no answer yet, the crowd can link together the people working around the world to find it. Our pockets and purses are full of digital silver bullets for killing the trillion-dollar vampires. So to the doubters, I say that maybe it is going to take a new mission to the moon to set our country back on the right path, but we already have the computing and communications power to make every American part of the mission as never before.

We may never wipe out all of the greedy bastards, but with our resolve and our digital technologies, we can reduce their numbers and minimize the damage they can inflict on our world. And we can do even more. As we implement the VICI code and revive American democracy, we can release the greatest forces for innovation, democracy, and prosperity that the world has ever seen.

I believe this is the great challenge for our time. In that spirit, I want to leave you with this parting thought. At the end of the Constitutional Convention in 1787, Benjamin Franklin was asked what kind of government he and the other Founding Fathers had just created. He replied, "A republic, if you can keep it."

I look forward to working with you to reach our goal.

Acknowledgments

I'd like to acknowledge those who wrote this book with me: G. F. Lichtenberg and Dr. Jeffrey Spees.

I'd like to acknowledge all of those who supported us while we wrote this book like Derek Evans, Audrey Benson, Steve Friedman, Chris Richards, and the Ratigan Family, not to mention all of those who have supported this endeavor from its beginning like Richard Chapman, Matt Winkler, Marty Schenker, John Raymond, Elliott Verner, Jason Del Col, Aprille Goodman, Lance Goodman, and John Melloy.

ACKNOWLEDGMENTS

Special acknowledgement is due to Meredith Fein Lichtenberg for supporting Greg in this year-long mission; to Jon Karp, Ben Loehnen, Richard Rhorer, Kelly Welsh, Jackie Seow, Gina DiMascia, Irene Kheradi, Eric Rayman, Jessica Abell, Sammy Perlmutter, Lisa Healy, and everyone at Simon & Schuster working to bring it to life; to Richard Pine at Inkwell Management; to Ken Sunshine and Marni Tomljanovic at Sunshine Sachs; to Alan Berger at CAA; and to the staff in Dr. Spees' laboratory at the University of Vermont who worked without their leader for a month so that Jeff could work with us on this book. Thanks, too, to Scott Buschkuhl at Hinterland for his work on the jacket and the diagrams and to Jim Hunt for drawing the book's political cartoons.

This book is possible because of the generous time given to us by experts such as Mohamed El-Erian and Bill Gross at Pimco, Dr. John Noseworthy at the Mayo Clinic, Salmon Kahn at the Kahn Academy, Mark Fisher at MBF Clearing, Susie Buffett at the Sherwood Foundation, Jimmy Williams at The Get Money Out Foundation, Gary Parr, Deputy Chairman at Lazard Freres, Christine Choi and Richard Branson at The Virgin Group, Michael Eisner at Tornante, Frank Aquila at Sullivan & Cromwell, Richard Grasso at Gladiator Holdings, Phil Griffin at MSNBC, Atul Gawande at *The New Yorker*, Nick Negroponte and Frank Moss at MIT, Andrew Jenks at MTV, Carl Icahn at Icahn Associates, Jon and Pete Najarian at Optionmonster, Mike Bloomberg at Bloomberg LP, Andrew Chapman and Marcus Samuelsson at the Samuelsson Group, Ed Rendell, former Pennsylvania governor, Dan Dimicco and Pat McFadden at Nucor Steel, T. Boone Pickens and Jay Rosser at BP Capital, Josh Fox, filmmaker of *Gasland*, Frank Islam, Ed Crego, and George Munoz who authored *Renewing the American Dream*, Barry

Ritholz at Fusion IQ, James Woolsey, former director of the CIA, Robert Kennedy, Jr., at the National Resources Defense Council, Bill Fleckenstein at Fleckenstein Capital, Arianna Huffington at the Huffington Post, Martin Bashir at MSNBC, and Deepak Chopra along with countless other solution seekers who show us every day all the new ways things can be done.

And finally to the truth squad who led the effort to turn the grand story told in this book into cold, hard, irrefutable fact: Matt Stoller, Gretchen Gavett, Brendan Crane, Megan Robertson, Betsy Korona, Brian Nerkowski, Mary Murphy, Tammy Caputo, Jesse Rodriguez, Sasha Walek, Nick Tuths, John Estrada, Chris Schwarz, Charlie Hitchens, and Dominic Palumbo.

Thank you all.

Index

Page numbers in *italics* refer to charts.

About the Author

DYLAN RATIGAN is the host of MSNBC's *The Dylan Ratigan Show*, an opinion-fueled daily broadcast program, and the podcast *Radio Free Dylan*. The creator of CNBC's *Fast Money* and formerly the coanchor of CNBC's *The Call* and *Closing Bell*, Ratigan started his career in print journalism and rose to become the global managing editor at Bloomberg. He has worked as a regular on-air contributor for ABC News and published articles in newspapers and magazines, including the *New York Times*, the *Washington Post*, the *Miami Herald*, and the *Chicago Tribune*. His coverage of the Enron scandal at CNBC earned him journalism's coveted Gerald Loeb Award.